The Black Creek stopping-house : and other stories

Nellie L. McClung

Nabu Public Domain Reprints:

THE BLACK CREEK STOPPING-HOUSE

AND

OTHER STORIES

BY

NELLIE L. McCLUNG

Author of "Sowing Seeds in Danny" and "The
Second Chance"

TORONTO
WILLIAM BRIGGS
1919

To the Pioneer Women of the West, who made life tolerable, and even comfortable, for the others of us; who fed the hungry, advised the erring, nursed the sick, cheered the dying, comforted the sorrowing, and performed the last sad rites for the dead;

The beloved Pioneer Women, old before their time with hard work, privations, and doing without things, yet in whose hearts there was always burning the hope of better things to come;

The godly Pioneer Women, who kept alive the conscience of the neighborhood, and preserved for us the best traditions of the race;

To these noble Women of the early days, some of whom we see no more, for they have entered into their inheritance, this book is respectfully dedicated by their humble admirer,

The Author.

*" Let me live in a house by the side of the road,
and be a friend of man."*

CONTENTS

THE BLACK CREEK STOPPING-HOUSE

The Black Creek Stopping-House

CHAPTER I.

THE OLD TRAIL.

When John Corbett strolled leisurely into the Salvation Army meeting in old Victoria Hall in Winnipeg that night, so many years ago now, there may have been some who thought he came to disturb the meeting.

There did not seem to be any atmospheric reason why Mr. Corbett or anyone else should be abroad, for it was a drizzling cold November night, and the streets were muddy, as only Winnipeg streets in the old days could be—none of your light-minded, fickle-hearted, changeable mud that is mud to-day and dust to-morrow, but the genuine, original, brush-defying, soap-and-water-proof, north star, burr mud, blacker than lampblack, stickier than glue!

Mr. Corbett did not come to disturb the meeting. His reason for attending lay in a perfectly legitimate desire to see for himself what it was all about, he being happily possessed of an open mind.

Mr. Corbett would do anything once, and if he liked it he would do it again. In the case of the Salvation Army meeting, he liked it. He liked the music, and the good fellowship, and the swing and the zip of it all. More still, he liked the blue-eyed Irish girl who sold *War Crys* at the door. When he went in he bought one; when he came out he bought all she had left.

The next night Mr. Corbett was again at the meeting. On his way in he bought all the *War Crys* the blue-eyed Irish girl had. Every minute he liked her better, and when the meeting was over and an invitation was given to the anxious ones to "tarry awhile," Mr. Corbett tarried. When the other cases had been dismissed Mr. Corbett had a long talk with the captain in charge.

Mr. Corbett was a gentleman of private means, though he was accustomed to explain his manner of making a livelihood, when questioned by magistrates and other interested persons, by saying he was employed in a livery stable. When further pressed by these insatiably curious people as to what his duties in the livery stable were, he always described his position as that of "chamber maid." Here the magistrates and other questioners thought that Mr. Corbett was disposed to be facetious, but he was perfectly sincere, and he had described his work more accurately than they gave him credit for. It might have been more illuminative if he had said that in the livery stable of Pacer and Kelly he did the " upstairs " work.

It was a small but well appointed room in which Mr. Corbett worked. It had an unobtrusive narrow stairway leading up to it. The only furniture it contained was several chairs and a round table with a well-concealed drawer, which opened with a spring, and held four packs and an assorted variety of chips! Its one window was well provided with a heavy blind. Here Mr. Corbett was able to accommodate any or all who felt that they would like to give Fortune a chance to be kind to them.

The night after Mr. Corbett had attended the Salvation Army meeting, his " upstairs " room was as dark inside as it always appeared to be on the outside. Two anxious ones, whose money was troubling them, had to be turned away disappointed. Mr. Corbett had left word downstairs that he was going out.

After Mr. Corbett had explained the situation to the Salvation Army captain, the captain took a day to consider. Then Mrs. Murphy, mother of Maggie Murphy who sold *War Crys*, was consulted. Mrs. Murphy had long been a soldier in the Army, and she had seen so many brands plucked from the burning that she was not disposed to discourage Mr. Corbett in his new desire to " do diff'rent."

Soon after this Mr. Corbett, in his own words, " pulled his freight " from the Brunswick Hotel, where he had been a long, steady boarder, and installed himself in the only vacant room in the Murphy house, having read the black and white card in the parlor window, which proclaimed " Furnished Rooms and Table Board," and regarding it as a providential opportunity for him to see Maggie Murphy in action !

Having watched Maggie Murphy wait on table in the daytime and sell *War Crys* at night for a week or more, Mr. Corbett decided he liked her methods. The way she poised a tray of teacups on her head proclaimed her a true artist.

At the end of two weeks Mr. Corbett stated his case to Mrs. Murphy and Maggie.

" I've a poor hand," he declared; " but I am willing to play it out if Maggie will sit opposite me and be my partner. I have only one gift— I'm handy with cards and I can deal myself three out of the four aces—but that's not much good to a man who tries to earn an honest living. I am willing to try work—it may be all right for anything I know. If Maggie will take me I'll promise to leave cards alone, and I'll do whatever she thinks I ought to do."

Maggie and her mother took a few days to consider. On one point their minds were very clear. If Maggie " took " him, he could not keep any of the money he had won gambling—he would have to start honest. Mr. Corbett had, fortunately, arrived at the same conclusion himself, so that point was easily disposed of.

" It ain't for us to be hard on anyone that's tryin' to do better," said Maggie's mother, as she rolled out the crust for the dried-apple pies. " He's wasted his substance, and wasted his days, but who knows but the Lord can use him yet to His honor and glory. The Lord ain't like us, havin' to wait until He gets everything to His own likin', but He can go ahead with whatever comes to His hand. He can do His work with poor tools, and it's well for Him He can, and well for us, too."

Maggie Murphy and John Corbett were married.

John Corbett got a job at once as teamster for a transfer company, and Maggie followed her mother's example and put a sign of " Table Board " in the window.

They lived in this way for ten years, and in spite of the dismal prognostications of friends, John Corbett worked industriously, and did not show any desire to return to his old ways! When he said he would do what Maggie told him it was not the rash promise of an eager lover, for Mr. Corbett was never rash, and the subsequent years showed that his purpose was honest to fulfil it to the letter.

Maggie, being many years his junior, could not think of addressing him by his first name, and she felt that it was not seemly to use the prefix, so again she followed her mother's example, and addressed him as her mother did Murphy, senior, as "Da."

It was in the early eighties that Maggie and John Corbett decided to come farther west. The cry of free land for the asking was coming to many ears, and at Maggie's table it was daily discussed. They sold out the contents of their house, and, purchasing oxen and a covered wagon, they made the long overland journey. On the bank of Black Creek they pitched their tent, and before a week had gone by Maggie Corbett was giving meals to hungry men, cooking bannocks, frying pork, and making coffee on her little sheet-iron camp-stove, no bigger than a biscuit-box.

The next year, when the railroad came to Brandon, and the wheat was drawn in from as far south as Lloyd's Lake, the Black Creek Stopping-House became a far-famed and popular establishment.

CHAPTER II.

THE HOUSE OF BREAD.

Across the level plain which lies between the valley of the Souris and the valley of the Assiniboine there ran, at this time, three trails. There was the deeply-rutted old Hudson Bay trail, over which went the fabulously heavy loads of fur long ago—grass-grown now and broken with badger holes; there was "the trail," hard and firm, in the full pride of present patronage, defying the invasion of the boldest blade of grass; and by the side of it, faint and shadowy, like a rainbow's understudy, ran "the new trail," strong in the certainty of being the trail in time.

For miles across the plain the men who follow the trail watch the steep outlying shoulder of the Brandon Hills for a landmark. When they leave the Souris valley the hills are blue with distance and seem to promise wooded slopes, and maybe leaping streams, but a half-day's journey dispels the illusion, for when the traveller comes near enough to see the elevation as it is, it is only a rugged bluff, bald and bare, and blotched with clumps of mangy grass, with a fringe of stunted poplar at the base.

BLACK CREEK STOPPING-HOUSE

After rounding the shoulder of the hill, the thick line of poplars and elms which fringe the banks of Black Creek comes into view, and many a man and horse have suddenly brightened at the sight, for in the shelter of the trees there stands the Black Creek Stopping-House, which is the half-way house on the way to Brandon. Hungry men have smelled the bacon frying when more than a mile away, and it is only the men who follow the trail who know what a heartsome smell that is. The horses, too, tired with the long day, point their ears ahead and step livelier when they see the whitewashed walls gleaming through the trees.

The Black Creek Stopping-House gave not only food and shelter to the men who teamed the wheat to market—it gave them good fellowship and companionship. In the absence of newspapers it kept its guests abreast with the times; events great and small were discussed there with impartial deliberation, and often with surprising results. Actions and events which seemed quite harmless, and even heroic, when discussed along the trail, often changed their complexion entirely when Mrs. Maggie Corbett let in the clear light of conscience on them, for even on the very edge of civilization there are still to be found finger-posts on the way to right living.

Mrs. Maggie Corbett was a finger-post, and more, for a finger-post merely points the way with its wooden finger, and then, figuratively, retires from the scene to let you think it over; but Maggie Corbett continued to take an interest in the case until it was decided to her entire satisfaction.

Black Creek, on whose wooded bank the Stopping-House stands, is a deep black stream which makes its way leisurely across the prairie between steep banks. Here and there throughout its length are little shallow stretches which show a golden braid down the centre like any peaceful meadow brook where children may with safety float their little boats, but Black Creek, with its precipitous holes, is no safe companion for any living creature that has not webbed toes or a guardian angel.

The banks, which are of a spongy black loam, grow a heavy crop of coarse meadow grass, interspersed in the late summer with the umbrella-like white clusters of water hemlock.

.   .   .   .

About a mile from the Stopping-House there stood a strange log structure, the present abode of Reginald and Randolph Brydon, late of H. M. Navy, but now farmers and homesteaders. The house was built in that form of architecture known as a "Red River frame," and the corners were finished in the fashion called "saddle and notch."

2   17

BLACK CREEK STOPPING-HOUSE

Whatever can be done to a house to spoil its appearance had been done to this one. There was a "join" in each side, which was intended, and a bulge which was accidental, and when the sailor brothers were unable to make a log lie comfortably beside its neighbor by using the axe, they resorted to long iron spikes, and when these split the logs, as was usually the case, they over-came the difficulty by using ropes.

What had brought the Brydon brothers to Manitoba was a matter of conjecture in the Black Creek neighborhood. Some said they probably were not wanted at home; others, with deeper meaning, said they probably *were* wanted at home; and, indeed, their bushy eyebrows, their fierce black eyes, the knives which they carried in their belts, and their general manner of living, gave some ground to this insinuation.

The Brydon brothers did not work with that vigor and zeal which brings success to the farmer. They began late and quit early, with numerous rests in between. They showed a delightfully child-like trust in Nature and her methods, for in the springtime, instead of planting their potatoes in the ground the way they saw other people doing it, they sprinkled them around the "fireguard," believing that the birds of the air strewed leaves over them, or the rain washed them in, or in some mysterious way they made a bed for themselves in the soil.

18

They bought a cow from one of the neighbors, but before the summer was over brought her back indignantly, declaring that she would give no milk. Randolph declared that he knew she had it, for she had plenty the last time he milked her, and that was several days ago—she should have more now. It came out in the evidence that they only took from the cow the amount of milk that they needed, reasoning that she had a better way of keeping it than they had. The cow's former owner exonerated her from all blame in the matter, saying that " Rosie " was all right as a cow; but, of course, she was " no bloomin' refrigerator!"

There was only one day in the week when the Brydon brothers could work with any degree of enjoyment, and that was on Sunday, when there was the added zest of wickedness. To drive the oxen up and down the field in full view of an astonished and horrified neighborhood seemed to take away in large measure from the " beastliness of labor," and then, too, the Sabbath calm of the Black Creek valley seemed to stimulate their imagination as they discoursed loudly and elaborately on the present and future state of the oxen, consigning them without hope of release to the remotest and hottest corner of Gehenna. But the complacent old oxen, graduates in the school of hard knocks and mosquitoes, winked solemnly, switched their tails and drowsed along unmoved.

The sailors had been doing various odd jobs around the house on Sundays ever since they came, but had not worked openly until one particular Sunday in May. All day they hoped that someone would come and stop them from working, or at least beg of them to desist, but the hot afternoon wore away, and there was no movement around any of the houses on the plain. The guardian of the morals of the neighborhood. Mrs. Maggie Corbett, had taken notice of them all right, but she was a wise woman and did not use militant methods until she had tried all others; and she believed that she had other means of teaching the sailor twins the advantages of Sabbath observance.

About five o'clock the twins grew so uproariously hungry they were compelled to quit their labors, but when they reached their house they were horrified to find that a wandering dog, who also had no respect for the Sabbath, had depleted their "grub-box," overlooking nothing but the tea and sugar, which he had upset and spilled when he found he did not care to eat them.

Then it was the oxen's turn to laugh, for the twins' wrath was all turned upon each other. Everything that they had said about the oxen, it seemed, was equally true of each other—each of them had confidently expected the other one to lock the door.

There was nothing to do but to go across to the Black Creek Stopping-House for supplies. Mrs. Corbett baked bread for them each week.

Reginald, with a gun on his shoulder, and rolling more than ever in his walk, strolled into the kitchen of the Stopping-House and made known his errand. He also asked for the loan of a neck-yoke, having broken his in a heated argument with the "starboard" ox.

Mrs. Corbett, with a black dress and white apron on, sat, with folded hands, in the rocking-chair. "Da" Corbett, with his "other clothes" on and his glasses far down on his nose, sat in another rocking-chair reading the life of General Booth. Peter Rockett, the chore boy, in a clean pair of overalls, and with hair-oil on his hair, sat on the edge of the wood-box twanging a Jew's-harp, and the tune that he played bore a slight resemblance to "Pull for the Shore."

Randolph felt the Sunday atmosphere, but, nevertheless, made known his errand.

"The bread is yours," said Mrs. Corbett, sternly; "you may have it, but I can't bake any more for you!"

"W'y not?" asked Reginald, feeling all at once hungrier than ever.

"Of course I am not saying you can help it," Mrs. Corbett went on, ignoring his question. "I suppose, maybe, you do the best you can. I believe everybody does, if we only knew it, and you haven't had a very good chance either, piratin' among the black heathen in the islands of the sea; but the Bible speaks plain, and old Captain Coombs often told us not to be unequally yoked with unbelievers, and I can't encourage Sunday-breakin' by cookin' for them that do it!"

"We weren't breakin', really we were only back-settin'," interposed Reginald, quickly.

"I don't wish to encourage Sabbath-breakin'," repeated Mrs. Corbett, raising her voice a little to prevent interruptions, "by bakin' for people who do it, or neighborin' with people who do it. Of course there are some who say that the amount of work that you and your brother do any day would not break the Sabbath." Here she looked hard at her man, John Corbett, who stirred uneasily. "But there is no mistakin' your meanin', and besides," Mrs. Corbett went on, "we have others besides ourselves to think of—there's the child," indicating the lanky Peter Rockett.

The "child" thus alluded to closed one eye— the one farthest from Mrs. Corbett—for a fraction of a second, and kept on softly teasing the Jew's-harp.

"Now you need not glare at me so fierce, you twin." Mrs. Corbett's voice was still full of Sunday calm. "I do not know which one of you you

are, but anyway what I say applies to you both.
Now take that look off your face and stay and
eat. I'll send something home to your other one,
too."

Having delivered her ultimatum on the subject of Sunday work, Mrs. Corbett became quite
genial. She heaped Reginald's plate with cold
chicken and creamed potatoes, and, mellowed by
them and the comfort of her well-appointed table,
he was prepared to renounce the devil and all his
works if Mrs. Corbett gave the order.

CHAPTER III.

THE SAILORS' REST.

WHEN Reginald reached home he found his brother in a state of mind bordering on frenzy, but when he shoved the basket which Mrs. Corbett had filled for him toward Randolph with the unnecessary injunction to " stow it in his hold," the lion's mouth was effectively closed. When he had finished the last crumb Reginald told him Mrs. Corbett's decree regarding Sunday work, and found that Randolph was prepared to abstain from all forms of labor on all days in the week if she wished it.

That night, after the twins had washed the accumulated stock of dishes, and put patches on their overalls with pieces of canvas and a sail needle, and performed the many little odd jobs which by all accepted rules of ethics belong to Sunday evening's busy work, they sat beside the fire and indulged in great depression of spirits!

" She can't live forever," Reginald broke out at last with apparent irrelevance. But there was no irrelevance—his remark was perfectly in order.

He was referring to a dear aunt in Bournemouth. This lady, who was possessed of "funds,"
had once told her loving nephews—the twins—
that if they would go away and stay away she
might—do something for them—by and by. She
had urged them so strongly to go to Canada that
they could not, under the circumstances, do other-
wise. Aunt Patience Brydon shared the delusion
that is so blissfully prevalent among parents and
guardians of wayward youth in England, that to
send them to Canada will work a complete re-
formation, believing that Canada is a good, kind
wilderness where iced tea is the strongest drink
known, and where no more exciting game than
draughts is ever played.

Aunt Patience, though a frail-looking little
white-haired lady, had, it seemed, a wonderful
tenacity of life.

"She'll slip her cable some day," Reginald declared soothingly. "She can't hold out much
longer—you know the last letter said she was
failin' fast."

"Failin' fast!" Randolph broke in impatiently
"It's us that's failin' fast! And maybe when
we've waited and waited, and stayed away for
'er, she'll go and leave it all to some Old Cats'
'Ome or Old Hens' Roost, or some other beastly
charity. I don't trust 'er—any woman that 'olds
on to life the way she does—'er with one foot in

the grave, and 'er will all made and everything
ready."

"Well, she can't last always," Reginald declared, holding firmly to this one bit of comfort.

The next news they got from Bournemouth
was positively alarming! She was getting better.
Then the twins lost hope entirely and decided to
treat Aunt Patience as one already dead—figuratively speaking, to turn her picture to the wall.

"Let her live as long as she likes," Reginald
declared, "if she's so jolly keen on it!"

When they decided to trust no more to the de-
ceitfulness of woman they turned to another
quarter for help, for they were, at this time, "un-
commonly low in funds."

It was Randolph who got the idea, one day
when he was sitting on the plow handle lighting
his pipe.

"Wot's the matter with us gettin' out Fred for
our farm pupil? He's got some money—they
say he married a rich man's daughter—and we've
got the experience!"

"He's only a 'alf-brother!" said Reginald, at
last, reflectively.

"That don't matter one bit to me," declared
Randolph, generously, "I'll treat him just the
same as I would you!"

Reginald shrugged his shoulders eloquently.

"What about his missus?" asked Reginald,
after a silence.

"She can come," Randolph said, magnanimously. "We'll build a piece to the house."

The more they talked about it the more enthusiastic they became. Under the glow of this new project they felt they could hurl contempt on Aunt Patience and her unnatural hold on life.

"I don't know but what I would rather take 'elp from the livin' than the dead, anyway," Reginald said, virtuously, that night before they went to bed.

"They're more h'apt to ask it back, just the same," objected Randolph.

"I was just goin' to say," Reginald began again, "that I'd just as soon take 'elp from the livin' as the dead, especially when there ain't no dead!"

They began at once to write letters to their long-neglected brother Fred, enthusiastically setting forth the charms of this new country. They dwelt on the freedom of the life, the abundance of game, and the view! They made a great deal of the view, and certainly there was nothing to obstruct it, for the prairie lay a dead level for ten miles north of them, only dotted here and there with little weather-bleached warts of houses like their own, where other optimists were trying to make a dint in the monotony.

The letters which went east every mail were splendid productions in their way, written with ease and eloquence, and utterly untrammeled by any regard for facts.

Their brother responded just as they hoped he would, and the twins were greatly delighted with the success of their plan.

Events of which the twins knew nothing favored their project and made Fred and his wife glad to leave Toronto. Evelyn Grant had bitterly estranged her father by marrying against his wishes. So the proposal from Randolph and Reginald that they come West and take the homestead near them seemed to offer an escape from much that was unpleasant. Besides, it was just at the time when so many people were hearing the call of the West.

At the suggestion of his brothers, Fred sent in advance the money to build a house on his homestead. But the twins, not wishing to make any mistake, or to have any misunderstanding with Fred, built it right beside their own. Fred sent enough money to have a frame building put up; but the twins decided that logs were more romantic and cheaper. It was a remarkable structure when they were through with it, stuck against their own house, as if by accident, and resembling in its irregularity the growth of a freak potato. Cables were freely used; binder twine served as hinges on the doors and also as latches.

They gave as a reason for sticking the new part against their own irregularly that they intended to use the alcoves for verandahs!

They agreed to put in Fred's crop for him—for a consideration; to put up hay; to buy oxen. Indeed, so many kindly offices did they agree to perform for him that Fred had advanced them, in all, nearly two thousand dollars.

The preparations were watched with great interest by the neighbors, and the probable outcome of it all was often a topic of conversation at the Black Creek Stopping-House.

CHAPTER IV.

FARM PUPILS.

JUNE in Manitoba, when the tender green of grass and leaf is bathed in the sparkling sunshine; when the first wild roses are spilling their perfume on the air, and the first orange lilies are lifting their glad faces to the sun; when the prairie chicken, intent on family cares, runs cautiously beside the road, and the hermit thrushes from the thickets drive their sweet notes into the quiet evening. It is a time to remember lovingly and with sweet gratitude; a time when the love of the open prairie overtakes us, and binds us fast in golden fetters. There is no hint of the cruel winter that is waiting just around the corner, or of the dull autumn drizzle closer still; there is nothing but peace and warmth and beauty.

As the old "Cheyenne," the only sidewheeler on the Assiniboine, churning the muddy water into creamy foam, made its way to the green shore at Curry's Landing, Fred and Evelyn Brydon, standing on the narrow deck, felt the grip of the place and the season. Even the captain's picturesque language, as he directed the activities of the " rousters " who pulled the boat ashore, seemed less like profanity and more like figure of speech.

The twins had made several unfruitful journeys to the Landing for their brother and his wife, for they began to go two days before the " Cheyenne " was expected, and had been going twice a day since, all of which had been carefully entered in their account book!

Their appearance as they stood on the shore, sneering at the captain's directions to his men from the superior height of their nautical experience, was warlike in the extreme, although they were clothed in the peaceful overalls and smock of the farmer and also had submitted to a haircut at the earnest instigation of Mrs. Corbett, who threatened to cut off all bread-making unless her wishes were complied with!

Evelyn, who had never seen her brothers-in-law, looked upon them now in wonder, and she could see their appearance was somewhat of a surprise to Fred, who had not seen them for many years, and who remembered them only as the heroes of his childhood days.

They greeted Fred hilariously, but to his wife they spoke timidly, for, brave as they were in facing Spanish pirates, they were timid to the point of flight in the presence of women.

As they drove home in the high-boxed wagon, the twins endeavored to keep up the breezy enthusiasm that had characterized their letters. They raved about the freedom of the West; they went into fresh raptures over the view, and almost deranged their respiratory organs in their praises of the air. They breathed in deep breaths of the ambient atmosphere, chewed it up with loud smacks of enjoyment, and then blew it out, snorting like whales. Evelyn, who was not without a sense of humor, would have enjoyed it all, and laughed *at* them, even if she could not laugh with them, if she could have forgotten that they were her husband's brothers, but it is very hard to see the humorous in the grotesque behavior of those to whom we are " bound by the ties of duty," if not affection.

A good supper at the Black Creek Stopping-House and the hearty hospitality of Mrs. Corbett restored Evelyn's good spirits. She noticed, too, that the twins tamed down perceptibly in Mrs. Corbett's presence.

Mrs. Corbett insisted on Fred and his wife spending the night at the Stopping-House.

" Don't go to your own house until morning," she said. " Things look a lot different when the sun is shining, and out here, you see, Mrs. Fred, we have to do without and forget so many things that we bank a lot on the sun. You people who live in cities, you've got gas and big lamps, and I guess it doesn't bother you much whether the sun rises or doesn't rise, or what he does, you're independent; but with us it is different. The sun is the best thing we've got, and we go by him considerable. Providence knows how it is with us, and lets us have lots of the sun, winter and summer."

Evelyn gladly consented to stay.

Mrs. Corbett, observing Evelyn's soft white hands, decided that she was not accustomed to work, and the wonder of how it would all turn out was heavy upon her kind Irish heart as she said goodbye to her next morning.

A big basket of bread and other provisions was put into the wagon at the last minute. "Maybe your stove won't be drawin' just right at the first," said Maggie Corbett, apologetically. As she watched Evelyn's hat of red roses fading in the distance she said softly to herself: "Sure I do hope it's true that He tempers the wind to the shorn lamb, tho' there's some that says that ain't in the Bible at all. But it sounds nice and kind anyway, and yon poor lamb needs all the help He can give her. Him and me; we'll have to do the best we can for her!"

Mrs. Corbett went over to see her new neighbor two or three days after. In response to her knock on the rough lumber door, a thin little voice called to her to enter, which she did.

On the bare floor stood an open trunk from which a fur-trimmed pale pink opera cloak hung carelessly. Beside the trunk in an attitude of homesickness huddled the young woman, hair dishevelled, eyes red. Her dress of green silk, embroidered stockings and beaded slippers looked out of place and at variance with her primitive surroundings.

When Mrs. Corbett entered the room she sprang up hastily and apologized for the untidiness of her house. She chattered gaily to hide the trouble in her face, and Mrs. Corbett wisely refrained from any apparent notice of her tears, and helped her to unpack her trunks and set the house to rights.

Mrs. Corbett showed her how to make a combined washstand and clothes press out of two soap boxes, how to make a wardrobe out of the head of the bed, and set the twin sailors at the construction of a cookhouse where the stove could be put.

When Mrs. Corbett left that afternoon it was a brighter and more liveable dwelling. Coming home along the bank of Black Creek, she was troubled in mind and heart for her new neighbor.

"This is June," she said to herself, "and wild roses are crowdin' up to her door, and the meadow larks are sittin' round all over blinkin' at the sun, and she has her man with her, and she ain't tired with the work, and her hands ain't cracked and sore, and she hasn't been there long enough to dislike the twins the way she will when she knows them better, and there's no mosquitoes, and she hasn't been left to stay alone, and still she cries! God help us! What will she do in the long drizzle in the fall, when the wheat's spoilin' in the shock maybe, and the house is dark, and her man's away—what *will* she do?"

Mrs. Brydon spent many happy hours that summer at the Stopping-House, and soon Mrs. Corbett knew all the events of her past life; the sympathetic understanding of the Irish woman made it easy for her to tell many things. Her mother had died when she was ten years old, and since then she had been her father's constant companion until she met Fred Brydon.

She could not understand, and so bitterly resented, her father's dislike of Fred, not knowing that his fond old heart was torn with jealousy. She and her father were too much alike to ever arrive at an understanding, for both were proud and quick-tempered and imperious, and so each day the breach grew wider. Just a word, a caress, an assurance from her that she loved him still, that the new love had not driven out the old, would have set his heart at rest, but with the cruel thoughtlessness of youth she could see only one side of the affair, and that her own.

At last she ran away and was married to the young man, whom her father had never allowed her to bring to see him, and the proud old man was left alone in his dreary mansion, brooding over what he called the heartlessness of his only child.

Mrs. Corbett, with her quick understanding, was sorry for both of them, and at every opportunity endeavored to turn Evelyn's thoughts towards home. Once, at her earnest appeal, after she had got the young woman telling her about how kind her father had been to her when her mother died, Evelyn consented to write him a letter, but when it was finished, with a flash of her old imperious pride, she tore it across and flung the pieces on the floor, then hastily gathered them up and put them in the stove.

One half sheet of the letter did not share the fate of the remainder, for Mrs. Corbett intercepted it and hastily hid it in her apron pocket. She might need it, she thought.

CHAPTER V.

THE PRAIRIE CLUB-HOUSE.

THE tender green of the early summer deepened and ripened into the golden tinge of autumn as over the Black Creek Valley the mantle of harvest was spread.

Only a small portion of the valley was under cultivation, for the oldest settler had been in only for three years; but it seemed as if every grain sowed had fallen upon good soil and gave promise of the hundredfold.

Across John Corbett's ten acres of wheat and forty acres of oats the wind ran waves of shadow all day long, and the pride of the land-owner thrilled Maggie Corbett's heart over and over again.

Not that the lady of the Stopping-House took the time to stand around and enjoy the sensation, for the busy time was coming on and many travellers were moving about and must be fed. But while she scraped the new potatoes with lightning speed, or shelled the green peas, all of her own garden, her thoughts were full of that peace and reverent gratitude that comes to those who plant the seed and see it grow.

37

BLACK CREEK STOPPING-HOUSE

It was a glittering day in early August; a light shower the night before had washed the valley clean of dust, and now the hot harvest sun poured down his ripening rays over the pulsating earth. To the south the Brandon Hills shimmered in a pale gray mirage. Over the trees which sheltered the Stopping-House a flock of black crows circled in the blue air, croaking and complaining that the harvest was going to be late. On the wire-fence that circled the haystack sat a row of red-winged blackbirds like a string of jet beads, patiently waiting for the oats to ripen and indulging in low-spoken but pleasant gossip about all the other birds in the valley.

Within doors Mrs. Corbett served dinner to a long line of stoppers. Many of the " boys " she had not seen since the winter before, and while she worked she discussed neighborhood matters with them, the pleasing sizzle of eggs frying on a hot pan making a running accompaniment to her words.

The guests at Mrs. Corbett's table were a typical pioneer group—homesteaders, speculators, machine men journeying through the country to sell machinery to harvest the grain not yet grown; the farmer has ever been well endowed with hope, and the machine business flourishes.

Mrs. Corbett could talk and work at the same time, her sudden disappearances from the room

38

as she replenished the table merely serving as
punctuation marks, and not interfering with the
thread of the story at all.

When she was compelled by the exigencies of
the case to be present in the kitchen, and there-
fore absent in the dining-room, she merely
elevated her voice to overcome distance, and
dropped no stitch in the conversation.

"New neighbor, is it, you are sayin', Tom?
'Deed and I have, and her the purtiest little
trick you ever saw—diamond rings on her, and
silk skirts, and plumes on her hat, and hair as
yalla as gold."

"When she comes over here I can't be doin'
my work for lookin' at her. She was brought up
with slathers of money." This came back from
the "cheek of the dure," where Mrs. Corbett was
emptying the tea leaves from the teapot. "But
the old man, beyant, ain't been pleased with her
since she married this Fred chap—he wouldn't
ever look at Fred, nor let him come to the house,
and so she ran away with him, and no one could
blame her either for that, and now her and the
old man don't write at all, at all—reach me the
bread plate in front of you there, Jim—and
there's bad blood between them. I can see,
though, her and the old man are fond o' one
another!"

"Is her man anything like the twin pirates?"
asked Sam Moggey from Oak Creek; "because

if he is I don't blame the old man for being mad
about it." Sam was helping himself to another
quarter of vinegar pie as he spoke.

Mrs. Corbett could not reply for a minute, for
she was putting a new bandage on Jimmy Mac-
Caulay's finger, and she had the needle and
thread in her mouth.

"Not a bit like them, Sam," she said, as soon
as she had the bandage in place, and as she put
in quick stitches; "no more like them than day
is like night—he's only a half-brother, and a lot
younger. He's a different sort altogether from
them two murderin' villains that sits in the
house all day playin' cards. He's a good, smart
fellow, and has done a lot of breakin' and
cleanin' up since he came. What he thinks of
the other two lads I don't know—she never says,
but I'd like fine to know."

"Sure, you'll soon know then, Maggie," said
"Da" Corbett, bringing in another platter of
bacon and eggs and refilling the men's plates
"Don't worry."

In the laugh that followed Maggie Corbett
joined as heartily as any of them.

"Go 'long with you, Da!" she cried; "sure
you're just as anxious as I am to know. We all
think a lot of Fred and Mrs. Fred," she went on.
bringing in two big dishes of potatoes; "and if
you could see that poor, precious lamb trying to
cook pork and beans with a little wisp of an

apron on, all lace and ribbons, and big diamonds on her fingers, you'd be sorry for her, and you'd say, 'What kind of an old tyrant is the old man down beyant, and why don't he take her and Fred back?' It's not wrastlin' round black pots she should be, and she's never been any place all summer only over here, for they've only the oxen, and altho' she never says anything, I'll bet you she'd like a bit of a drive, or to get out to some kind of a-doin's, or the like of that."

While Mrs. Corbett gaily rattled on there was one man at her table who apparently took no notice of what she said.

He was a different type of man from all the others. Dark complexioned, with swarthy skin and compelling black eyes, he would be noticeable in any company. He was dressed in the well-cut clothes of a city man, and carried himself with a certain air of distinction.

Happening to notice the expression on his face, Mrs. Corbett suddenly changed the conversation, and during the remainder of the meal watched him closely with a puzzled and distrustful look.

When the men had gone that day and John Corbett came in to have his afternoon rest on the lounge in the kitchen, he found Maggie in a self-reproachful mood.

"Da," she began, "the devil must have had a fine laugh to himself when he saw the Lord puttin' a tongue in a woman's head. Did ye hear me to-day, talking along about that purty young thing beyant, and Rance Belmont takin' in every word of it? Sure and I never thought of him bein' here until I noticed the look on that ugly mug of his, and mind you, Da, there's people that call him good-lookin' with that heavy jowl of his and the hair on him growin' the wrong way on his head, and them black eyes of his the color of the dirt in the road. They do say he's just got a bunch of money from the old country, and he's cuttin' a wide swath with it. If I'd kept me mouth shut he'd have gone on to Brandon and never knowed a word about there being a purty young thing near. But I watched him hitchin' up, and didn't he drive right over there; and I tell you, Da, he means no good."

"Don't worry, Maggie," John Corbett said, soothingly. "He can't pick her up and run off with her. Mrs. Fred's no fool."

"He's a divil!" Maggie declared with conviction. "Mind you, Da, there ain't many that can put the comaudher on me, but Rance Belmont done it once."

Mr. Corbett looked up with interest and waited for her to speak.

"It was about the card-playin'. You know I've never allowed a card in me house since I -had a house, and never intended to, but the last

day Rance Belmont was here—that was away
last spring, when you were away—he begins to
play with one of the boys that was in for dinner.
Right in there on the sewin'-machine in plain
sight of all of us I saw them, and I wiped me
hands and tied up me apron, and I walked in,
and says I, 'I'll be obliged to you, Mr. Belmont,
to put them by,' and I looked at him, stiff as
pork. 'Why, certainly, Mrs. Corbett," says he,
smilin' at me as if I had said somethin' pleasant.
I felt a little bit ashamed, and went on to sort of
explain about bein' brought up in the Army and
all that, and he talked so nice about the Army
that you would have thought it was old Major
Morris come back again from the dead, and
pretty soon he had me talkin' away to him and
likin' him; and says he, 'I was just going to
show Jimmy here a funny trick that can be done
with cards, but,' says he, 'if Mrs. Corbett ob-
jects I wouldn't offend her for the world!' Now
here's the part that scares me, Da—me, Maggie
Murphy, that hates cards like I do the divil;
says I to him, 'Oh, go on, Mr. Belmont; I don't
mind at all!' Now what do you think of that,
Da?"

John Corbett sat thinking, but he was not
thinking of what Maggie thought he was thinking. He was wondering what trick it was that
Rance Belmont had showed Jimmy Peters!

CHAPTER VI.

THE COUNTER-IRRITANT.

WHEN Fred Brydon made the discovery that his two brothers spent a great deal of their time in the pleasant though unprofitable occupation of card-playing with two or three of the other impecunious young men of the neighborhood, he remonstrated with them on this apparent waste of time. When he later discovered that they were becoming so engrossed in the game that they had but little time to plant, sow or reap, or do any of the things incidental to farm life, he became very indignant indeed.

The twins naturally resented any such interference from their farm pupil. They told him that he was there to learn farming, and not to give advice to his elders.

Nearly everyone agrees that card playing is a pleasant and effective way of killing time for people who wait for a long delayed train at a lonely wayside station. This is exactly the position in which the twins found themselves. So, while Aunt Patience, of Bournemouth, tarried and procrastinated, her loving nephews across the sea, thinking of her night and day, waited with as good grace as they could and played the game!

Unlike the twins, Fred Brydon liked hard work, and applied himself with great energy to the work of the farm, determined to disprove his angry father-in-law's words that he would never make a success of anything.

The fact that the twins were playing for money gave Fred some uneasy moments, and the uncomfortable suspicion that part of his money was being used in this way kept growing upon him.

He did not mention any of these things to Evelyn, for he knew it was hard for her to keep up friendly relations with Reginald and Randolph, and he did not want to say anything that would further predispose her against them.

However, Evelyn, with some of her father's shrewdness, was arriving at a very correct estimate of the twins without any help from anyone.

The twins had enjoyed life much better since the coming of their brother and his wife. They quite enjoyed looking out of the fly-specked window at their brother at work with the oxen in the fields. Then, too, the many flattering remarks made by their friends in regard to their sister-in-law's beauty were very grateful to their ears.

BLACK CREEK STOPPING-HOUSE

One day, in harvest time, when something had gone wrong with their binder, and Fred had sent to Brandon for a new knotter, the twins refused to pay for it when it came, telling him that he could pay for it himself. Fred paid for it and worked all afternoon without saying anything, but that evening he came into their part of the house and told them he wanted a detailed statement of how his money had been spent.

The twins were thoroughly hurt and indignant. Did he think they had cheated him? And they asked each other over and over again, " Did anybody ever hear of such ingratitude?"

The next day Evelyn made a remark which quite upset them. She told them that if Fred did all the work he should have more than half the crop.

The twins did not like these occurrences. Instinctively they felt that a storm was coming. They began to wonder what would be the best way to avoid trouble.

The prairie-dwellers have a way of fighting a prairie fire which is very effective. When they see the blue veil of smoke lying close to the horizon, or the dull red glare on the night sky, they immediately start another fire to go out and meet the big fire!

Some such thought as this was struggling in the twins' brains the day that Rance Belmont came over from the Stopping-House, and in his graceful way asked Mrs. Brydon to go driving with him, an invitation which Fred urged her to accept. When the drive was over and Rance came in to the twins' apartments, and on their invitation had a game with them and lost, they were suddenly smitten with an idea. They began to see how it might be possible to start another fire!

CHAPTER VII.

LADIES' DAY AT THE STOPPING-HOUSE.

THE glory of the summer paled and faded; the crimson and gold of the harvest days had fled before the cold winds of autumn, and now the trees along the bank of the creek stood leafless and bare, trembling and swaying as if in dread of the long winter that would soon be upon them. The harvest had been cut and gathered in, and now, when the weather was fine, the industrious hum of the threshing-machine came on the wind for many miles, and the column of blue smoke which proclaimed the presence of a " mill " shot up in all directions.

At the Black Creek Stopping-House the real business of the year had begun, for every day heavily-loaded wheat wagons wound slowly over the long trail on their way to Brandon, and the Stopping-House became the foregathering place of all the farmers in the settlement. At noon the stable yard presented a lively appearance as the " boys " unhitched their steaming teams and led them to the long, straggling straw-roofed stables. The hay that John Corbett had cut on the meadows of Black Creek and stacked beside

48

the stables was carried in miniature stacks which completely hid the man who carried them into the mangers, while the creaking windlass of the well proclaimed that the water-troughs were being filled. The cattle who foraged through the straw stack in the field near by always made the mistake of thinking that they were included in the invitation, much to the disgust of Peter Rockett, the chore boy, who drove them back with appropriate remarks.

Inside of the Stopping-House the long dining-room, called "the room," was a scene of great activity. The long oilcloth-covered table down the centre of the "room" was full of smoking dishes of potatoes and ham and corned beef, and piled high with bread and buns; tin teapots were at each end of the table and were passed from hand to hand. There were white bowls filled with stewed prunes and apricots and pitchers of "Goldendrop" syrup at intervals down the table.

Table etiquette was fairly well observed—the person who took the last of the potatoes was in duty bound to take the dish out to the kitchen and replenish it from the black pot which stood on its three legs on the back of the kitchen stove. The same rule applied to the tea and the bread. Also when one had finished his meal the correct plan of procedure was to gather up his plate, knife and fork and cup and saucer and carry them out to the kitchen, where Mrs. Corbett or Peter Rockett hastily washed them to be ready for the next one.

When entering the Black Creek dining-room with the purpose of having a meal there were certain small conventions to be observed. If a place was already set, the newcomer could with impunity sit down and proceed with the order of business; if there was no place set, but room for a place to be set, the hungry one came out to the kitchen and selected what implements he needed in the way of plate and knife and proceeded to the vacancy; if there was not a vacant place at the table, the newcomer retired to the window and read the *Northern Messenger* or the *War Cry*, which were present in large numbers on the sewing-machine. But before leaving the table conversation zone, it was considered perfectly legitimate to call out in a loud voice: "Some eat fast, some eat long, and some eat both ways," or some such bright and felicitous remark.

It was a bitter cold day in November—one of those dark, cold days with a searching wind, just before the snow comes. In Mrs. Corbett's kitchen there was an unusual bustle and great excitement, for the women from the Tiger Hills were there—three of them on their way to Brandon. Mrs. Corbett said it always made her nervous to cook for women. You can't fool them on a bad pudding by putting on a good sauce, the way you can a man. But Mrs. Corbett admitted it was good to see them anyway.

There was Mrs. Berry and her sister, Miss Thornley, and Mrs. Smith. They had ridden fifteen miles on a load of wheat, and had yet another fifteen to go to reach their destination. In spite of a long, cold and very slow ride, the three ladies were in splendid condition, and as soon as they were thawed out enough to talk, and long before their teeth stopped chattering, they began to ask about Mrs. Corbett's neighbor, young Mrs. Brydon, in such a way, that, as Mrs. Corbett afterwards explained to Da Corbett, "you could tell they had heard something."

"Our lads saw her over at the Orangemen's ball in Millford, and they said Rance Belmont was with her more than her own man," said Mrs. Berry, as she melted the frost from her eyebrows by holding her face over the stove.

"Oh, well," Mrs. Corbett said, "I guess all the young fellows were makin' a lot of her, but sure there's no harm in that."

Miss Thornley was too busy examining her feet for possible frostbites to give in her contribution just then, but after she had put her coldest foot in a wash-basin of water she said, "I don't see how any woman can go the length of her toe with Rance Belmont, but young Mrs. Brydon went to Brandon with him last week, for my sister's husband heard it from somebody that had seen them. I don't know how she can do it."

Mrs. Corbett was mashing potatoes with a gem-jar, and without stopping her work she said: "Oh, well, Miss Thornley, it's easy for you and me to say we would not go out with Rance Belmont, but maybe that's mostly because we have never had the chance He's got a pretty nice way with him, Rance has, and I guess if he came along now with his sorrel pacer and says to you, 'Come on, Miss Thornley,' you would get on that boot and stocking in two jiffies and be off with him like any young girl!"

Miss Thornley mumbled a denial, and an angry light shone in her pale blue eyes.

Mrs. Smith was also full of the subject, and while she twisted her hair into a small "nub" about the size, shape and color of a peanut, she expressed her views.

"It ain't decent for her to be goin' round with Rance Belmont the way she does, and they say at the dance at Millford she never missed a dance. Since Rance has got his money from England he hasn't done a thing but play cards with them twins and take her round. I don't see how her man can put up with it, but he's an awful easy-goin' chap—just the kind that wouldn't notice anything wrong until he'd come home some night and find her gone. I haven't one bit of respect for her."

"Oh, now, Mrs. Smith, you're too hard on her. She's young and pretty and likes a good time." Mrs. Corbett was giving her steel knives a quick rub with ashes out of deference to the lady stoppers. "It's easy enough for folks like us," waving her knife to include all present, "to be very respectable and never get ourselves talked about, for nobody's askin' us to go to dances or fly around with them, but with her it's different. Don't be hard on her! She ain't goin' to do anything she shouldn't."

But the ladies were loath to adopt Mrs. Corbett's point of view. All their lives nothing had happened, and here was a deliciously exciting possible scandal, and they clung to it.

"They say the old man Grant is nearly a millionaire, and he's getting lonely for her, and is pretty near ready to forgive her and Fred and take them back. Wouldn't it be awful if the old man should come up here and find she'd gone with Rance Belmont?"

Mrs. Berry looked anxiously around the kitchen as if searching for the lost one.

"Oh, don't worry," declared Mrs. Corbett; "she ain't a quitter. She'll stay with her own man; they're happy as ever I saw two people."

"If she did go," Miss Thornley said, sentimentally, "if she did go, do you suppose she'd leave a note pinned on the pin-cushion? I think they mostly do!"

When the ladies had gone that afternoon, and while Mrs. Corbett washed the white ironstone dishes, she was not nearly so composed and confident in mind as she pretended to be.

"Don't it beat the band how much they find out? I often wonder how things get to be known. I do wish she wouldn't give them the chance to talk, but she's not the one that will take tellin'—too much like her father for that—and still I kind o' like her for her spunky ways. Rance is a divil, but she don't know that. It is pretty hard to tell what ought to be done. This is surely work for the Almighty, and not for sinful human beings!"

That night Mrs. Corbett took her pen in hand. Mrs. Corbett was more at home with the potato-masher or the rolling-pin, but when duty called her she followed, even though it involved the using of unfamiliar tools.

She wrote a lengthy letter to Mr. Robert Grant, care of The Imperial Lumber Company, Toronto, Ontario:

"Dear and respected sir," Mrs. Corbett wrote, "I take my pen in hand to write you a few things that maybe you don't know but ought to know, and to tell you your daughter is well, but homesick sometimes hoping that you are enjoying the same blessings as this leaves us at

present. Your daughter is my neighbor and a
blessed girl she is, and it is because I love her so
well that I am trying to write to you now, not
being handy at it, as you see; also my pen spits.
As near as I can make out you and her's cut off
the same cloth; both of you are touchy and
quick, and, if things don't suit you, up and coming. But she's got a good heart in her as ever
I see. One day she told me a lot about how
good you were to her when her mother died, and
about the prayer her mother used to tell her
to say: 'Help papa and mamma and Evelyn to
be chums.' When she came to that she broke
right down and cried, and says she to me, 'I
haven't either of them now!' If you'd a-seen
her that day you'd have forgot everything only
that she was your girl. Then she sat down and
wrote you a long letter, but when she got done
didn't she tear it up, because she said you told
her you wouldn't read her letters. I saved a
bit of the letter for you to see, and here it is.
We don't any of us see what made you so mad
at the man she got—he's a good fellow, and puts
up with all her high temper. She's terrible
like yourself, excuse me for saying so and meaning no harm. If she'd married some young
scamp that was soaked in whiskey and cigarettes you'd a-had something to kick about. I
don't see what you find in him to fault. Maybe
you'll be for telling me to mind my own busi-

ness, but I am not used to doing that, for I like to take a hand any place I see I can do any good, and if I was leaving my girl fretting and lonely all on account of my dirty temper, both in me and in her, though for that she shouldn't be blamed, I'd be glad for someone to tell me. If you should want to send her a Christmas present, and she says you never forgot her yet, come yourself. It's you she's fretting for. You can guess it's lonely for her here when I tell you she and me's the only women in this neighborhood, and I keep a stopping-house, and am too busy feeding hungry men to be company for anyone.

"Hoping these few lines will find you enjoying the same blessings,

"Yours respectively,

"MAGGIE CORBETT."

The writing of the letter took Mrs. Corbett the greater part of the afternoon, but when it was done she felt a great weight had been lifted from her heart. She set about her preparations for the evening meal with more than usual speed.

Going to the door to call Peter Rockett, she was surprised to see Rance Belmont, with his splendid sorrel pacer, drive into the yard. He came into the house a few minutes afterwards and seemed to be making preparations to stay for supper.

A sudden resolve was formed in Mrs. Corbett's mind as she watched him hanging up his coat and making a careful toilet at the square looking-glass which hung over the oilcloth-covered soap box on which stood the wash-basin and soap saucer. She called to him to come into the pantry, and while she hurriedly peeled the potatoes she plunged at once into the subject.

"Rance," she began, "you go to see Mrs. Brydon far too often, and people are talking about it."

Rance shrugged his shoulders.

"Now, don't tell me you don't care, or that it's none of my business, though that may be true."

"I would never be so lacking in politeness, however true it might be!" he answered, rolling a cigarette.

Mrs. Corbett looked at him a minute, then she broke out, "Oh, but you are the smooth-tongued gent!—you'd coax the birds off the bushes; but I want to tell you that you are not doing right hanging around Mrs. Brydon the way you do."

"Does she object?" he asked, in the same even tone, as he slowly struck a match on the sole of his boot.

"She's an innocent little lamb," Mrs. Corbett cried, "and she's lonely and homesick, and you've taken advantage of it. That poor lamb can't stand the prairie like us old pelters that's weatherbeaten and gray and toughened—she ain't made for it—she was intended for diamond rings and drawing-rooms, and silks and satins."

Rance Belmont looked at her, still smiling his inexplicable smile.

"I can supply them better than she is getting them now," he said.

Mrs. Corbett gave an exclamation of surprise.

"But she's a married woman," she cried, "and a good woman, and what are you, Rance? Sure you're no mate for any honest woman, you black-hearted, smooth-tongued divil!" Mrs. Corbett's Irish temper was mounting higher and higher, and two red spots burned in her cheeks. "You know as well as I do that there's no happiness for any woman that goes wrong. That woman must stand by her man, and he's a good fellow, Fred is; such a fine, clean, honest lad, he never suspects anyone of being a crook or meanin' harm. Why can't you go off and leave them alone, Rance? They were doin' fine before you came along. Do one good turn, Rance, and take yourself off."

"You ask too much, Mrs. Corbett. I find Mrs. Brydon very pleasant company, and Mr. Fred does not object to my presence."

"But he would if he knew how the people talk about it."

"That is very wrong of them, and entirely unavoidable," Rance answered, calmly. "But the opinion of the neighbors has never bothered me yet," he continued; "why should it in this instance?"

Mrs. Corbett's eyes flashed ominously.

"Do you know what I'd do if it was my girl you were after?" she asked, pausing in her work and fixing her eyes on him.

"Something very unpleasant, I should say, by the tone of your voice—and, by the way, you are pointing your potato knife at me—"

Mrs. Corbett with an effort controlled her temper.

"I believe, Mrs. Corbett, you would do me bodily injury. What a horrible thought, and you a former officer in the Salvation Army!" Rance was smiling again and enjoying the situation. "What a thrilling headline it would make for the Brandon *Sun*: 'The Black Creek Stopping-House scene of a brutal murder. Innocent young man struck down in his youth and beauty.' You make me shudder, Mrs. Corbett, but you look superb when you rage like that; really, you women interest me a great deal. I am so fond of all of you!"

"You're a divil, Rance!" Mrs. Corbett repeated again. "But you ain't goin' to do that blessed girl any harm—she's goin' to be saved from you some way."

"Who'll do it, I wonder?" Rance seemed to triumph over her.

"There is One," said Maggie Corbett, solemnly, "who comes to help when all other help fails."

"Who's that?" he asked, yawning.

Maggie Corbett held up her right hand.

"It is God!" she said slowly.

Rance laughed indulgently. "A myth—a name—a superstition," he sneered; "there is no God any more."

"There is a God," she said, slowly and reverently, for she was Maggie Murphy now, back to the Army days when God walked with her day by day, "and He can hear a mother's prayer, and though I was never a mother after the flesh, I am a mother now to that poor girl in the place of the one that's gone, and I'm askin' Him to save her, and I've got me answer. He will do it."

There was a gleam in her eyes and a white glow in her face that made Rance Belmont for one brief moment tremble, but he lighted another cigarette and with a bow of exaggerated politeness left the room.

The days that followed were anxious ones for Mrs. Corbett. Many stoppers sat at her table as the Christmas season drew near, and many times she heard allusions to her young neighbor which filled her with apprehension. She had carefully counted the days that it would take her letter to reach its destination, and although there had been time for a reply, none came.

CHAPTER VIII.

SHADOWS OF THE NIGHT.

It was a wind-swept, chilly morning in late November, and Evelyn Brydon, alone in the silent little house, stood at the window looking listlessly at the dull gray monochrome which stretched before her.

The unaccustomed housework had roughened and chapped her hands, and the many failures in her cooking experiments, in spite of Mrs. Corbett's instructions, had left her tired and depressed, for a failure is always depressing, even if it is only in the construction of the things which perish.

This dark morning it seemed to her that her life was as gray and colorless as the bleached-out prairie—the glamor had gone from everything.

She and Fred had had their first quarrel, and Fred had gone away dazed and hurt by the things she had said under the stress of her anger. He was at a loss to know what had gone wrong with Evelyn, for she had seemed quite contented all the time. He did not know how the many little annoyances had piled up on her; how the utter loneliness of the prairie, with its monotonous sweep of frost-killed grass, the deadly sameness, and the perpetual silence of the house, had so worked upon her mind that it required but a tiny spark to cause an explosion.

The spark he had supplied himself when he had tried to defend his brothers from her charges. All at once Evelyn felt herself grow cold with anger, and the uncontrolled hasty words, bitterer than anything she had ever thought, utterly unjust and cruel, sprang to her lips, and Fred, stung to the quick with the injustice of it, had gone away without a word.

It was with a very heavy heart that he went to his work that day; but he had to go, for he was helping one of the neighbors to thresh, and every dry day was precious, and every man was needed.

All day long Evelyn went about the house trying to justify herself. A great wave of self-pity seemed to be engulfing her and blotting out every worthier feeling.

The prairie was hateful to her that day, its dull gray stretches cruel and menacing, and a strange fear of it seemed to possess her.

All day she tried to busy herself about the house, but she worked to no purpose, taking up things and laying them down again, forgetting what she was going to do with them; strange whispering voices seemed to sound in the room behind her, trying to tell her something—to warn her—and it was in vain that she tried to shake off their influence. Once or twice she caught a glimpse of a black shadow over her shoulder, just a reflecting vanishing glimpse, and when she turned hastily round there was nothing there, but the voices, mocking and gibbering, were louder than ever.

She wished Fred would come. She would tell him that she hadn't meant what she said.

As the afternoon wore on, and Fred did not make his appearance, a sudden deadly fear came over her at the thought of staying alone. Of course the twins occupied the other half of the house, and to-night, at least, she was glad of their protection.

Suddenly it occurred to her that she had heard no sound from their quarters for a long time. She listened and listened, the silence growing more and more oppressive, until at last, overcoming her fears, she went around and tried the door. Even the voices of her much-despised brothers-in-law would be sweet music to her ears.

The door was locked and there was no response to her knocks.

An old envelope stuck in a sliver in the door bore the entry in lead-pencil, "Gone Duck Shooting to Plover Slough," for it was the custom of the twins to faithfully chronicle the cause of

their absence and their probable location each
time they left home, to make it easy to find them
in the event of a cablegram from Aunt Patience's
solicitors!

Evelyn turned away and ran back to her
own part of the house. She hastily barred the
door.

The short autumn day was soon over. The
sun broke out from the dull gray mountain of
clouds and threw a yellow glare on the colorless
field. She stood by the window watching the
light as it faded and paled and died, and then
the shades of evening quickly gathered. Turning again to replenish the fire, the darkness of
the room startled her. There was a shadow
under the table like a cave's mouth. Unaccustomed sounds smote her ear; the logs in the
house creaked uncannily, and when she walked
across the floor muffled footfalls seemed to follow her.

She put more wood in the stove and tried to
shake off the apprehensions which were choking
her. She lit the lamp and hastily drew down
the white cotton blind and pinned it close to
keep out the great pitiless staring Outside, which
seemed to be peering in at her with a dozen
white, mocking, merciless faces.

In the lamp's dim light the shadows were
blacker than ever; the big packing-box threw a

shadow on the wall that was as black as the mouth of a tunnel in a mountain.

She noticed that her stock of wood was running low, and with a mighty effort of the will she opened the door to bring in some from a pile in the yard. Stopping a minute to muster up her courage, she waited at the open door. Suddenly the weird cry of a wolf came up from the creek bank, and it was a bitter, lonely, insistent cry.

She slammed the door, and coming back into the room, sank weak and trembling into a chair. A horror grew upon her until the beads of perspiration stood upon her face. Her hands grew numb and useless, and the skin of her head seemed stiff and frozen. Her ears were strained to catch any sound, and out of the silence there came many strange noises to torment her overstrained senses.

She thought of Mrs. Corbett at the Stopping-House, and tried to muster courage to walk the distance, but a terrible fear held her to the spot.

The fire died out, and the room grew colder and colder, but huddled in a chair in a panic of fear she did not notice the cold. Her teeth chattered; spots of light danced before her tightly-shut eyes. She did not know what she was afraid of; a terrible nameless fear seemed to be clutching at her very heart. It was the living, waking counterpart of the nightmare that had made horrible her childhood nights—a gripping, overwhelming fear of what might happen.

Suddenly something burst into the room—the terrible something that she had been waiting for. The silence broke into a thousand screaming voices. She slipped to the floor and cried out in an agony of terror.

There was a loud knocking on the door, and then through the horrible silence that followed there came a voice calling to her not to be afraid.

She staggered to the door and unbarred it, and heard someone speak again a blessed human voice.

The door opened, and she found herself looking into the face of Rance Belmont, and her fear-tortured eyes gave him a glad welcome.

She seized him by the arm, holding to him as a child fear-smitten in the night will hold fast to the one who comes in answer to his cries.

Rance Belmont knew how to make the most, yet not too much, of an advantage. He soothed her fears courteously, gently; he built up the fire; he made her a cup of tea; there was that strange and subtle influence in all that he said and did that made her forget everything that was unpleasant and be happy in his presence.

A perfect content grew upon her; she forgot her fears—her loneliness—her quarrel with

Fred; she remembered only the happy company of the present.

Under the intoxication of the man's presence she ceased to be the tired, discouraged, irritable woman, and became once more the Evelyn Grant whose vivacity and wit had made her conspicuous in the brightest company.

She tried to remind herself of some of the unpleasant things that neighborhood gossip said of Rance Belmont—of Mrs. Corbett's dislike of him —but in the charm of his presence they all faded into vague unrealities.

There was flattery, clever, hidden flattery, which seemed like adoration, in every word he spoke, every tone of his voice, every glance of his coal-black eyes, that seemed in some way to atone for the long, gray, monotonous days that had weighed so heavily upon her spirits.

"Are you always frightened when you are left alone?" he asked her. Every word was a caress, the tone of his voice implying that she should never be left alone, the magnetism of his presence assuring her that she would never be left alone again.

"I was never left alone in the evening before," she said. "I thought I was very brave until to-night, but it was horrible—it makes me shudder to think of it."

"Don't think!" he said gently.

67

" Fred thought the twins would be here, I know, or he would not have stayed away," Evelyn said, wishing to do justice to Fred, and feeling indefinitely guilty about something.

" The twins are jolly good company,—oh, I say!" laughed Rance, in tones so like her brothers-in-law that Evelyn laughed delightedly. It was lovely to have someone to laugh with.

" But where are the heavenly twins to-night?"

" I suppose they saw a flock of ducks going over, or heard the honk-honk of wild geese," she answered. " It does not take much to distract them from labor—and they have a soul above it, you know."

Rance Belmont need not have asked her about the twins; he had met them on their way to the Plover Slough and had given Reginald the loan of his gun; he had learned from them that Fred, too, was away.

" But if dear Aunt Patience will only lift her anchor all will yet be well, and the dear twins will not need to be bothered with anything so beastly as farm-work." His tone and manner were so like the twins that Evelyn applauded his efforts. Then he told her the story of the cow, and of how the twins, endeavoring to follow the example of some of the Canadians whom they had seen locking their wagon-wheels with a chain when going down the Souris hill, had made a slight mistake in the location of the chain and hobbled the oxen, with disastrous results.

When he looked at his watch it was nine o'clock.

"I must go," he said, hastily rising; "it would hardly do for me to be found here!"

"What do you mean?" she asked in surprise.

"What do you suppose your husband would say if he came home and found me here?"

Evelyn flushed angrily.

"My husband has confidence in me," she answered proudly. "I don't know what he thinks of you, but I know what he thinks of me, and it would make no difference what company he found me in, he would never doubt me. I trust him in the same way. I would believe his word against that of the whole world."

She held her handsome head high when she said this.

Rance Belmont looked at her with a dull glow in his black eyes.

"I hope you are right," he said, watching the color coming in her face.

"I am right," she said after a pause, during which she had looked at him defiantly. He was wise enough to see he had made a false move and had lost ground in her regard.

"I think you had better go," she said at last. "I do not like that insinuation of yours that your presence here might be misconstrued. Yes, I want you to go. I was glad to see you; I was never so glad to see anyone; I was paralyzed with fear; but now I am myself again, and I am sure Fred will come home."

There was a sneering smile on his face which she understood and resented.

"In that case I had better go," he said.

"That is not the reason I want you to go. I tell you again that Fred would not believe that I was untrue to him. He believes in me utterly." She drew herself up with an imperious gesture and added: "I am worthy of his trust."

Rance Belmont thought he had never seen her so beautiful.

"I will not leave you," he declared. "Forgive me for speaking as I did. I judged your husband by the standards of the world. I might have known that the man who won you must be different from other men. It was only for your sake that I said I must go. I care nothing for his fury. If it were the fury of a hundred men I would stay with you; just to be near you, to hear your sweet voice, to see you, is heaven to me."

Evelyn sprang to her feet indignantly as he arose and came towards her.

Just at that moment the door opened, and Fred Brydon, having heard the last words, stood face to face with them both!

70

CHAPTER IX.

HIS EVIL GENIUS.

WHEN Fred Brydon went to his work that morning, smarting from the angry words that Evelyn had hurled at him, everyone he met noticed how gloomy and burdened he seemed to be; how totally unlike his former easy good-nature and genial cheerfulness was his strange air of reserve.

They thought they knew the cause, and told each other so when he was not listening.

When he came into the kitchen to wash himself at noon he heard one of the men say to another in an aside: " He'll be the last one to catch on."

He paid no particular attention to the sentence at the time, but it stuck in his memory.

The day was fine and dry, and the thresher was run at the top of its speed. One more day would finish the stacks, and as this was the last threshing to be done in the neighborhood, the greatest effort was put forth to finish it before the weather broke.

They urged him to stay the night—they would begin again at daylight—the weather was so uncertain.

He thought, of course, that the twins were safely at home, and Evelyn had often said that she was not afraid to stay. He had consented to stay, when all at once the weather changed.

The clouds had hung low and heavy all day, but after sundown a driving wind carrying stray flakes of snow began to whistle around the stacks. The air, too, grew heavy, and a feeling of oppression began to be evident.

The pigs ran across the yard carrying a mouthful of straw, and the cattle crowded into the sheds. Soon the ground was covered with loose snow, which began to whirl in gentle, playful eddies. The warmth of the air did not in any way deceive the experienced dwellers on the plain, who knew that the metallic whistle in the wind meant business.

The owner of the threshing machine covered it up with canvas, and all those who had been helping, as soon as they had supper, started to make the journey to their homes. It looked as if a real Manitoba blizzard was setting in.

In spite of the protestations of all the men, Fred did not wait for his supper, but set out at once on the three-mile walk home.

Evelyn's hasty words still stung him with the sense of failure and defeat. If Evelyn had gone back on him what good was anything to him?

Walking rapidly down the darkening trail, his thoughts were very bitter and self-reproachful;

he had done wrong, he told himself, to bring her
to such a lonely place—it would have been better
for Evelyn if she had never met him—she had
given up too much for his sake.

He noticed through the drifting storm that
there was something ahead of him on the trail,
and, quickening his steps, he was surprised to
overtake his two brothers leisurely returning
from their duck hunt.

"Why did you two fellows leave when you
knew I was away? You know that Evelyn will
be frightened to be left there all alone."

Instantly all his own troubles vanished at the
thought of his wife left alone on the wide prairie

His brothers strongly objected to his words.

"We don't 'ave to stay to mind 'er, do we?"
sneered Reginald.

"Maybe she ain't alone, either," broke in Ran
dolph, seeing an opportunity to turn Fred's
wrath in another direction.

"What are you driving at?" asked Fred in
surprise.

"Maybe Rance Belmont has dropped in again
to spend the evenin'—he usually does when
you're away!"

"You lie!" cried Fred, angrily.

"We ain't lyin'," declared Randolph. "Every
body knows it only you."

The words were no sooner said than Fred fell
upon him like a madman. Randolph roared

lustily for help, and Reginald valiantly strove to save him from Fred's fury. But they re treated before him as he rained his blows upon them both.

Then Reginald, finding that he was no match for Fred in open conflict, dodged around behind him, and soon a misty dizziness in his head told Fred that he had been struck by something heavier than hands. There was a booming in his ears and he fell heavily to the road.

The twins were then thoroughly frightened Here was a dreadful and unforeseen possibility.

They stood still to consider what was to be done.

"It was you done it, remember," said Ran dolph to Reginald.

"But I done it to save you!" cried Reginald indignantly, "and you can't prove it was me People can't tell us apart."

"Anyway," said Reginald, "everybody will blame it on Rance Belmont if he is killed—and see here, here's the jolly part of it. I'll leave Rance's gun right beside him. That'll fix the guilt on Rance!"

"Well, we won't go home; we'll go back and stay in the shootin'-house at the Slough, and then we can prove we weren't home at all, and there'll be no tracks by mornin', anyway."

The twins turned around and retraced their steps through the storm, very hungry and very

cross, but forgetting these emotions in the pres
ence of a stronger one—fear.

But Fred was not killed, only stunned by Reg
inald's cowardly blow. The soft flakes melting
on his face revived him, and sitting up he looked
about him trying to remember where he was
Slowly it all came to him, and stiff and sore, he
got upon his feet. There were no signs of the
twins, but to this Fred gave no thought; his
only anxiety was for Evelyn, left alone on such
a wild night.

When he entered his own house with Rance
Belmont's words ringing in his ears, he stood
for a moment transfixed. His brother's words
which he had so hotly resented surged over him
now with fatal conviction; also the words he had
heard at the threshing, " He'll be the last one to
catch on," came to him like the flash of lightning
that burns and uproots and destroys.

His head swam dizzily and lights danced be
fore his eyes. He stood for a moment without
speaking. He was not sure that it wasn't all a
horrible dream.

If he had looked first at Evelyn, her honest
face and flashing eyes would have put his un
worthy suspicions to flight. But Rance Belmont
with his fatal magnetic presence drew his gaze
Rance Belmont stood with downcast eyes, the
living incarnation of guilt. It was all a pose, of

course, but Rance Belmont, with his deadly gift of being able to make any impression he wished made a wonderful success of the part he had all at once decided to play.

Looking at him, Fred's smouldering jealousy burst into flame.

There was an inarticulate sound in his throat and striding forward he landed a smashing blow on Rance Belmont's averted face.

" Oh, Fred!" Evelyn cried, springing forward ' for shame!—how could you!—how dare you!—"

" Don't talk to me of shame!" Fred cried, his face white with anger.

" Don't blame her," Rance said in a low voice. He made no attempt to defend himself

In her excitement Evelyn did not notice the sinister significance of his words and what they implied. She was conscious of nothing only that Fred had insulted her by his actions, and her wrath grew as terrible as her husband's.

She caught him by the shoulder and compelled him to look at her.

" Fred," she cried, " do you believe—do you dare to believe this terrible thing?"

She shook him in her rage and excitement.

Rance Belmont saw that Fred would be convinced of her innocence if he did not gain his attention, and the devil in him spoke again, soft, misleading, lying words, part truth, yet all false, leaving no chance for denial.

"Don't blame her—the fault has all been mine," he interposed again.

In her blind rage again Evelyn missed the significance of his words. She was conscious of one thought only—Fred had not immediately craved her pardon. She shook and trembled with uncontrollable rage.

"I hate you, Fred!" she cried, her voice sounding thin and unnatural. "I hate you! One minute ago I believed you to be the noblest man on earth; now I know you for an evil-minded, suspicious, contemptible dog!—a dog!—a cur! My father was right about you. I renounce you forever!"

She pulled the rings from her finger and flung them against the window, cracking the glass across. "I will never look on your face again, I hope. This is my reward, is it, for giving up everything for you? I boasted of your trust in me a minute ago, but you have shamed me; you have dragged my honor in the dust, but now I am free—and you may believe what you please!"

She turned to Rance Belmont.

"Will you drive me to Brandon to-night?" she asked.

She put on her coat and hat without a word or a look at the man, who stood as if rooted to the ground.

Then opening the door she went out quickly, and Rance Belmont, with something like triumph on his black face, quickly followed her, and Fred Brydon, bruised in body and stricken in soul, was left alone in his desolate house.

CHAPTER X.

DA'S TURN.

THE wind was whistling down the Black
Creek Valley, carrying heavy flakes of snow that
whirled and eddied around them, as Rance Belmont and Evelyn made their way to the Stopping-House. The stormy night accorded well
with the turmoil in Evelyn's brain. One point
she had decided—she would go back to her
father, and for this purpose she asked her companion if he would lend her one hundred dollars.
This he gladly consented to do.

He was discreet enough to know that he must
proceed with caution, though he felt that in getting her separated from her husband and so
thoroughly angry with him that he had made
great progress. Now he believed that if he
could get her away from the Stopping-House his
magnetic influence over her would bring her entirely under his power.

But she had insisted on going in to the Stopping-House to see Mrs. Corbett and tell her what
she was going to do. It was contrary to Evelyn's
straightforwardness to do anything in an under-
handed way, and she felt that she owed it to Mrs.

79

Corbett, who had been her staunch friend, to tell her the truth of the story, knowing that many versions of it would be told.

Mrs. Corbett was busy setting a new batch of bread, and looked up with an exclamation of surprise when they walked into the kitchen, white with snow. It staggered Mrs. Corbett somewhat to see them together at that late hour, but she showed no surprise as she made Mrs Brydon welcome.

"I am going away, Mrs. Corbett," Evelyn began at once.

"No bad news from home, is there?" Mrs Corbett asked anxiously.

"No bad news from home, but bad news here Fred and I have quarrelled and parted for ever!"

Mrs. Corbett drew Evelyn into the pantry and closed the door. She could do nothing, she felt, with Rance Belmont present.

"Did you quarrel about him?" she asked, jerking her head towards the door.

Evelyn told her story, omitting only Rance Belmont's significant remarks, which indeed she had not heard.

Mrs. Corbett listened attentively until she was done.

"Ain't that just like a man, poor, blunderin' things they are. Sure and it was just his love for you, honey, that made him break out so jealous!"

"Love!" Evelyn broke in scornfully. "Love should include trust and respect—I don't want love without them. How dare he think that I would do anything that I shouldn't? Do I look like a woman who would go wrong?"

"Sure you don't, honey!" Mrs. Corbett soothed her, "but you know Rance Belmont is so smooth-tongued and has such a way with him that all men hate him, and the women like him too well. But what are you goin' to do, dear? Sure you can't leave your man."

"I have left him," said Evelyn. "I am going to Brandon now to-night in time for the early train. Rance Belmont will drive me."

Something warned Mrs. Corbett not to say all that was in her heart, so she temporized.

"Sure, if I were you I wouldn't go off at night —it don't look well. Stay here till mornin'. The daylight's the best time to go. Don't go off at night as if you were doin' something you were ashamed of. Go in broad daylight."

"What do I care what people say about me?" Evelyn raged again. "They can't say any worse than my husband believes of me. No—I am going—I want to put distance between us; I just came in to say good-bye and to tell you how it happened. I wanted you and Mr. Corbett to

know the truth, for you have been kind friends
to me, and I'll never, never forget you."

" I'd be afraid you'd never get to Brandon to-
night, honey." Mrs. Corbett held her close, de-
termining in her own mind that she would lock
her in the pantry if there was no other way of
detaining her. " Listen to the wind—sure it's
layin' in for a blizzard. I knew that all day.
The roads will be drifted so high you'd never get
there, even with the big pacer. Stay here to-
night just to oblige me, and you can go on in the
morning if it's fit."

Meanwhile John Corbett had been warning
Rance Belmont that the weather was unfit for
anyone to be abroad, and the fact that George
Sims, the horse trader from Millford, and Dan
Lonsbury, had put in for the night, made a splendid argument in favor of his doing the same
Rance Belmont had no desire to face a blizzard
unnecessarily, particularly at night, and the
storm was growing thicker every minute. So
after consulting with Evelyn, who had yielded
to Mrs. Corbett's many entreaties, he agreed to
remain where he was for the night. Evelyn went
at once to the small room over the kitchen, which
Mrs. Corbett kept for special guests, and as she
busied herself about the kitchen Mrs. Corbett
could hear her pacing up and down in her excitement.

DA'S TURN

Mrs. Corbett hastily baked biscuits and "buttermilk bread" to feed her large family, who, according to the state of the weather and the subsequent state of the roads, might be with her for several days, and while her hands were busy, her brain was busier still, and being a praying woman, Maggie Corbett was looking for help in the direction from which help comes.

The roaring of the storm as it swept past the house, incessantly mourning in the mud chimney and sifting the snow against the frosted windows, brought comfort to her anxious heart, for it reminded her that dominion and majesty and power belong to the God whom she served.

When she put the two pans of biscuits in the oven she looked through the open door into the "Room," where her unusual number of guests were lounging about variously engaged.

Rance Belmont smoked cigarettes constantly and shuffled the cards as if to read his fate therein. He would dearly have loved a game with some one, for he had the soul of a gambler, but Mrs. Corbett's decree against card-playing was well known.

Dan Lonsbury, close beside the table lamp, read a week-old copy of the Brandon *Times*. George Sims, the horse-dealer, by the light of his own lantern, close beside him on the bench, pared his corns with minute attention to detail.

BLACK CREEK STOPPING-HOUSE

Under the wall lamp, which was fastened to the window frame, Da Corbett, in his cretonne-covered barrel-chair of home manufacture, read the *War Cry,* while Peter Rockett, on his favorite seat, the wood-box, played one of the Army tunes on his long-suffering Jew's-harp.

"They can't get away as long as the storm lasts, anyway," Mrs. Corbett was thinking, thankful even for this temporary respite, "but they'll go in the mornin' if the storm goes down, and I can't stop them—vain is the help of man."

Suddenly Mrs. Corbett started as if she had heard a strange and disturbing noise; she threw out her hands as if in protest. She sat still a few moments holding fast to the kitchen table in her excitement; her eyes glittered, and her breath came short and fast.

She went hurriedly into the pantry, fearful that her agitation might be noticed. In her honest soul it seemed to her that her plan, so terrible, so daring, so wicked, must be sounding now in everybody's ears.

In the darkness of the pantry she tried to think it out. Was it an inspiration from heaven, or was it a suggestion of the devil? One minute she was imploring Satan to "get thee behind me," and the next minute she was thanking God and whispering Hallelujahs! A lull in the storm drove her to immediate action.

84

DA'S TURN

John Corbett came out into the kitchen to see what was burning, for Maggie had forgotten her biscuits.

When the biscuits were attended to she took " Da " with her into the pantry, and she said to him, " Da, is it ever right to do a little wrong so that good will come of it?"

She asked the question so impersonally that John Corbett replied without hesitation: " It is never right, Maggie."

" But, Da," she cried, seizing the lapel of his coat, " don't you mind hearin' o' how the priests have given whiskey to the Indians when they couldn't get the white captives away from them any other way? Wasn't that right?"

" Sure and it was; at a time like that it was right to do anything—but what are you coming at, Maggie?"

" If Rance Belmont lost all the money he has on him, and maybe ran a bit in debt, he couldn't go away to-morrow with her, could he? She thinks he's just goin' to drive her to Brandon, but I know him—he'll go with her, sure—she can't help who travels on the train with her— and how'll that look? But if he were to lose his money he couldn't travel dead broke, could he, Da?"

" Not very far," agreed Da, " but what are you coming at, Maggie ? Do you want me to go through him?" He laughed at the suggestion.

85

"Ain't there any way you can think of, Da—no, don't think—the sin is mine and I'll take it fair and square on my soul. I don't want you to be blemt for it—Da, listen—" she whispered in his ear.

John Corbett caught her in his arms.

"Would I? Would I? Oh, Maggie, would a duck swim?" he said, keeping his voice low to avoid being heard in the other room.

"Don't be too glad, Da; remember it's a wicked thing I'm askin' you to do; but, Da, are you sure you haven't forgot how?"

John Corbett laughed. "Maggie, when a man learns by patient toil to tell the under side of an ace he does not often forget, but of course there is always the chance, that's the charm of it—nobody can be quite sure."

"I've thought of every way I can think of," she said, after a pause, "and this seems to be the only way. I just wish it was something I could do myself and not be bringing black guilt on your soul, but maybe God'll understand. Maybe it was so that you'd be ready for to-night that He let you learn to be so handy with them. Sure Ma always said that God can do His work with quare tools; and now, Da, I'll slip off to bed, and you'll pretend you're stealin' a march on me, and he'll enjoy himself all the more if he thinks he's spitin' me. Oh, Da, I wish I knew it was right —maybe it's ruinin' your soul I am, puttin' you up to such wickedness, but I'll be prayin' for you as hard as I can."

Da looked worried. "Maggie, I don't know about the prayin'—I was always able to find the card I needed without bein' prayed for."

"Oh, I mean I'll pray it won't hurt you. I wouldn't interfere with the game, for I don't know one card from another, and I'm sure the Lord don't either, but it's your soul I'm thinkin' of and worried about. I'll slip down with the green box—there's more'n a hundred dollars in it. And now good-bye, Da—go at him, and God bless you—and play like the divil!"

Mr. John Corbett slowly folded up the *War Cry* and placed it in his pocket, and when Maggie brought down the green box with their earnings in it he emptied its contents in his pocket, and then, softly humming to himself, he went into the other room.

The wind raged and the storm roared around the Black Creek Stopping-House all that night, but inside the fire burned bright in the box-stove, and an interested and excited group sat around the table where Rance Belmont and John Corbett played the game! Peter Rockett, with his eyes bulging from his head, watched his grave employer cut and deal and gather in the stakes, with as much astonishment as if that dignified gentleman had walked head downward on the ceiling. Yet John Corbett proceeded with the game, as grave and solemn as when he asked a blessing at the table. Sometimes he hummed snatches of Army tunes, and sometimes Rance Belmont swore softly, and to the anxious ear which listened at the stovepipe-hole above, both sounds were of surpassing sweetness!

CHAPTER XI.

THE BLIZZARD.

WHEN the door closed behind Rance Belmont and Evelyn, Fred sank into a chair with the whole room whirling dizzily around him. Why had the world gone so suddenly wrong?

His head was quite clear now, and only the throbbing hurt on the back of his head reminded him of Reginald's cowardly blow. But his anger against his brothers had faded into apathy in the presence of this new trouble which seemed to choke the very fountains of his being.

One terrible fact smote him with crushing force—Evelyn had left him and gone with Rance Belmont. She said she hoped she would never see him again—that she was done with him—and her eyes had blazed with anger and hatred —and she had stepped in between him and the miserable villain whom he would have so dearly loved to have beaten the life out of.

He tried to rage against her, but instead he could think of nothing but her sweet imperiousness, her dazzling beauty, her cheerfulness under all circumstances, and her loyalty to him.

She had given up everything for him—for his sake she had defied her father, renounced all

share in his great wealth, suffered the hard-
ships and loneliness of the prairie, all for him.

Her workbag lay on the table, partly open.
It seemed to call and beckon to him. He took
it tenderly in his hands, and from its folds there
fell a crumpled sheet of paper. He smoothed
it out, and found it partly written on in Evelyn's
clear round hand.

He held it to the light eagerly, as one might
read a message from the dead. Who was
Evelyn writing to?

"*When you ask me to leave my husband you
ask me to do a dishonorable and cowardly thing.
Fred has never*"—the writing ceased abruptly.
Fred read it again aloud, then sprang to his
feet with a smothered exclamation. Only one
solution presented itself to his mind. She had
been writing to Rance Belmont trying to with-
stand his advances, trying to break away from
his devilish influence. She had tried to be true
to herself and to him.

Fred remembered then with bitter shame the
small help he had given her. He had wronged
her when he struck Rance Belmont.

One overwhelming thought rose out of the
chaos of his mind—she must be set free from
the baneful influence of this man. If she were
not strong enough to resist him herself, she must
be helped, and that help must come from him—
he had sworn to protect her, and he would do it

THE BLIZZARD

There was just one way left to him now. Fred's face whitened at the thought, and his eyes had an unnatural glitter, but there was a deadly purpose in his heart.

In his trunk he found the Smith and Wesson that one of the boys in the office had given him when he left, and which he had never thought of since. He hastily but carefully loaded it and slipped it into his pocket. Then reaching for his snowy overcoat, which had fallen to the floor, and putting the lamp in the window, more from habit than with any purpose, he went out into the night.

The storm had reached its height when Fred Brydon, pulling his cap down over his ears, set out on his journey. It was a wild enough night to turn any traveller aside from his purpose, but Fred Brydon, in his rage, had ceased to be a man with a man's fears, a man's frailties, and had become an avenging spirit, who knew neither cold nor fatigue. A sudden stinging of his ears made him draw his cap down more closely, but he went forward at a brisk walk, occasionally breaking into a run.

He had but one thought in his mind—he must yet save Evelyn. He had deserted her in her hour of need, but he would yet make amends.

The wind which sang dismally around him reminded him with a sickening blur of homesickness of the many pleasant evenings he and

91

Evelyn had spent in their little shack, with the same wind making eerie music in the pipe of the stove. Yesterday and to-day were separated by a gulf as wide as death itself.

He had gone about three miles when he heard a faint halloo come down the wind. It sounded two or three times before the real significance of it occurred to him, so intent was he upon his own affairs. But louder and more insistent came the unmistakable call for help.

A fierce temptation assailed Fred Brydon. He must not delay—every minute was precious— to save Evelyn, his wife, was surely more his duty than to set lost travellers on their way again. Besides, he told himself, it was not a fiercely cold night—there was no great danger of any person freezing to death; and even so, were not some things more vital than saving people from death, which must come sooner or later? Then down the wind came the cry again —a frightened cry—he could hear the words— "Help! help! for God's sake!" Something in Fred Brydon's heart responded to that appeal. He could not hurry by unheeding.

Guided by the calls, he turned aside from his course and made his way through the choking storm across the prairie.

The cries came nearer, and Fred shouted in reply—words of impatient encouragement. No rescuer ever went to his work with a worse grace.

A large, dark object loomed faintly through the driving storm.

" What's the matter?" called Fred, when he was within speaking distance.

" I'm caught—tangled up in some devilish thing," came back the cry.

Fred hurried forward, and found a man, almost covered with snow, huddled beside a haystack, his clothing securely held by the barbs of the wire with which the stack was fenced.

" You're stuck in the barbed wire," said Fred, as he removed his mittens and with a good deal of difficulty released the man from the close grip of the barbs.

" I hired a livery-man at Brandon to bring me out, and his bronchos upset us and got away from him. He walked them the whole way—the roads were heavy—and then look at what they did! I came over here for shelter—the driver ran after the team, and then these infernal fish-hooks got hold of me—what are they, anyway?"

Fred explained.

" This is surely a God-forsaken country that can jerk a storm like this on you in November," the older man declared, as Fred carefully dusted the snow off him, wondering all the time what he was going to do with him.

" Where are you going?" Fred asked, abruptly.

"I want to get to the Black Creek Stopping-House. How far am I from there now?"

"About three miles," said Fred.

"Well, I guess I can walk that far if you'll show me the road."

Fred hesitated.

"I am going to Brandon," he said.

"What is any sane man going to Brandon to-night for?" the stranger cried, impatiently. "Great Scott! I thought I was the only man who was a big enough fool to be out to-night. The driver assured me of that several times. I guess there's a woman in the case with you, too."

"Did you meet anyone?" Fred asked, quickly.

"Not a soul! I tell you you and I are the only crazy ones to-night."

Fred considered a minute.

"I'll take you on your way," he said.

The stranger suddenly remembered something. "I'm a good bit obliged to you, young man, whoever you are. I guess I'd have been here all night if you hadn't come along and heard me. I was beginning to get chilly, too. Is this a blizzard?"

"Yes, I guess it is," Fred answered, shortly, "and it's not improving any, so I guess we had better hurry on."

It was much easier going with the wind, and at first the older man, helped along by Fred, made good progress. Fred knew that every minute the drifts were growing higher and the road harder to keep.

The night grew colder and darker, and the storm seemed to thicken.

"Pretty hard going for an old man of sixty," the stranger said, stopping to get his breath. The storm seemed to choke him.

Soon he begged to be let rest, and when Fred tried to start him again he experienced some difficulty. The cold was getting into his very bones, and was causing a fatal drowsiness.

Fred told him this and urged him to put forth his greatest efforts. They were now but a mile from Fred's house. Every few minutes the light in the window glimmered through the storm, the only ray of light in the maze of whirling snow which so often thickened and darkened and blotted it out altogether.

When they were about half a mile from the house, the old man, without warning, dropped into the snow and begged Fred to go on without him. He was all right, he declared, warm and comfortable, and wanted to rest.

"You'll freeze to death!" Fred cried. "That's the beginning of it."

"Feel very comfortable," the old man mumbled.

Fred coaxed, reasoned, entreated, but all in vain. He shook the old man, scolded, threatened, but all to no purpose.

There was only one thing to be done.

Fred threw off his own coat, which was a heavy one, and picked the old man up, though he was no light weight, and set off with him.

But the man objected to being carried, and, squirming vigorously, slipped out of Fred's arms, and once more declared his intention of sleeping in the snow.

With his frozen mitten Fred dealt him a stinging blow on the cheek which made him yell with pain and surprise.

" Do what I tell you!" cried Fred.

The blow seemed to rouse him from his stupor, and he let Fred lead him onward through the storm.

When they arrived at Fred's house he put the old man in a rocking-chair, first removing his snowy outer garments, and made sure that he had no frost-bites. Then hastily lighting the fire, which had burned itself out, he made coffee and fried bacon.

When the old man had taken a cup of the coffee he began to take an interest in his surroundings.

" How did I get here?" he asked. " The last thing I remember I was sitting down, feeling very drowsy, and someone was bothering me to get up. Did I get up?"

" Not until I lifted you," said Fred.

"Did you carry me?" the other man asked in surprise.

"I did until you kicked and squirmed so I couldn't hold you."

"What did you do then?" queried his visitor, tenderly feeling his sore cheek.

"I slapped you once, but you really deserved far more," said Fred, gravely.

"What did I do then?"

"You got up and behaved yourself so nicely I was sorry that I hadn't slapped you sooner!"

The old man laughed to himself without a sound.

"What's your name?" he asked.

While this dialogue had been in progress Fred had been studying his companion closely, with a growing conviction that he knew him. He was older, grayer, and of course the storm had reddened his face, but Fred thought he could not be mistaken.

The old man repeated the question.

"Brown!" said Fred, shortly, giving the first name he could think of.

"You're a strapping fine young fellow, Brown, even if you did hit me with your hard mitt, and I believe I should be grateful to you."

"Don't bother," said Fred shortly.

"I will bother," the old man cried, imperiously, with a gesture of his head that Fred knew well;

"I will bother, and my daughter will thank you, too."

"Your daughter!" Fred exclaimed, turning his back to pick out another stick for the stove.

"Yes, my girl, my only girl—it's her I came to see. She's living near here. I guess you'd know her: she's married to a no-good English-man, a real lizzie-boy, that wouldn't say boo to a goose!"

Fred continued to fix the fire, poking it un-necessarily. He was confident that Evelyn's father would not recognize him with his crop of whiskers and sunburnt face. His mind was full of conflicting emotions.

"Maybe you know him," said the old man. "His name is Brydon. They live somewhere near the Stopping-House."

"I've not lived here long," said Fred, evasive-ly, "but I've heard of them."

The comfort and security of the warm little shack, as well as the good meal Fred had given him, had loosened the old man's tongue.

"I never liked this gent. I only saw him once, but it don't take me long to make up my mind. He carried a cane and had his monogram on his socks—that was enough for me—and a red tie on him, so red you'd think his throat was cut. I says to myself, 'I don't want that shop window Judy round my house,' but Evelyn thought he was the best going. Funny thing that that girl was the very one to laugh at dudes before that, but she stuck it out that he was a fine chap. She's game, all right, my girl is. She stays right with the job. I wrote and told her to come on back and I'd give her every cent I have—but she pitched right into me about not asking Fred. Here's her letter. Oh, she's a spunky one!" He was fumbling in his pockets as he spoke. Drawing out a long pocketbook, he took out a letter. He deliberately opened the envelope and read. Fred with difficulty held back his hand from seizing it.

"Listen to this how she lit into me: ' When you ask me to leave my husband you ask me to do a dishonorable thing—' "

Fred heard no more—he hung on to the seat of his chair with both hands, breathing hard, but the old man took no notice of him and read on:

" ' Fred is in every way worthy of your respect, but you have been utterly unjust to him from the first. I will enjoy poverty and loneliness with him rather than endure every pleasure without him.' "

Fred's world had suddenly righted itself—he saw it all now—this was the man she was writing to—this was the man who had tried to induce her to leave him.

"I haven't really anything against this Fred chap—maybe his clothes were all right. I was brought up in the lumber business, though, and

I don't take to flowered stockings and mono-
grams—I kept wondering how he'd look in overalls! What was really wrong with me—and
you'll never know how it feels until you have a
girl of your own, and she leaves you—was that
I was jealous of the young gent for taking my
girl when she was all I had."

Fred suddenly understood many things; a
fellow feeling for the old man filled his heart,
and in a flash he saw the past in an entirely different light.

He broke out impetuously, " She thinks of you
the same as ever, I know she does—" then, seeing
his mistake, he said, " I know them slightly, and
I've heard she was lonely for you."

" Then why didn't she tell me? She has always kept up these spunky letters to me, and said
she was happy, and all that—she liked to live
here, she said. What's this Fred fellow like?"
The old man leaned toward him confidentially.

" Oh, just so-so," Fred answered, trying to
make the stove take more wood than it was ever
intended to take. " I never had much use for
him, and I know people wondered what she saw
in him."

The old man was glad to have his opinion sus-
tained, and by a local authority, too.

" It wasn't because he hadn't money that I
objected to him—it wasn't that, for I have a
place in my business where I need a smart, up-

to-date chap, and I'd have put him there quick, but he didn't seem to have any snap in him—too polite, you know—the kind of a fellow that would jump to pick up a handkerchief like as if he was shot out of a gun. I don't care about money, but I like action. Now, if she had taken a fancy to a brown-faced chap like you I wouldn't have cared if he hadn't enough money to make the first payment on a postage stamp. I kinda liked the way you let fly at me when I was acting contrary with you out there in the storm. But, tell me, how does this Fred get on? Is he as green as most Englishmen?"

"He's green enough," Fred agreed, "but he's not afraid of work. But come now, don't you want to go to bed? I can put you up for the night, what there's left of it; it's nearly morning now."

The old man yawned sleepily, and was easily persuaded to go to bed.

When the old man was safely out of the way Fred put his revolver back where he had found it. The irony of the situation came home to him —he had gone out to kill, but in a mysterious way it had been given to him to save instead of take life. But what good was anything to him now?—the old man had come one day too late.

At daylight, contrary to all expectations, the storm went down, only the high packed drifts giving evidence of the fury of the night before.

As soon as the morning came Fred put on his
father-in-law's coat, having left his in the snow,
and went over to the Black Creek Stopping-
House. Mrs. Corbett was the only person who
could advise him.

He walked into the kitchen, which was never
locked, just as Mrs. Corbett, carrying her boots
in her hand as if she were afraid of disturbing
someone, came softly down the stairs.

Mrs. Corbett had determined to tell Fred what
a short-sighted, jealous-minded man he was when
she saw him, but one look at his haggard face—
for the events of the previous night were telling
on him now—made her forget that she had any
feeling toward him but sympathy. She read the
question in his eyes which his lips were afraid to
utter.

" She's here, Fred, safe and sound," she whispered.

" Oh, Mrs. Corbett," he whispered in return,
" I've been an awful fool! Did she tell you?
Will she ever forgive me, do you think?"

" Ask her!" said Mrs. Corbett, pointing up the
narrow stairs.

CHAPTER XII.

WHEN THE DAY BROKE.

ALL night long the tide of fortune ebbed and flowed around the table where Rance Belmont and John Corbett played the game which is still remembered and talked of by the Black Creek old settlers when their thoughts run upon old times.

Just as the daylight began to show blue behind the frosted panes, and the yellow lamplight grew pale and sickly, Rance Belmont rose and stretched his stiffened limbs.

" I am sorry to bring such a pleasant gathering to an end," he said, with his inscrutable smile, " but I believe I am done." He was searching through his pockets as he spoke. " Yes, I believe the game is over."

" You're a mighty good loser, Rance," George Sims declared with admiration.

The other men rose, too, and went out to feed their horses, for the storm was over and they must soon be on the road.

When John Corbett and Rance Belmont went out into the kitchen, Maggie Corbett was chopping up potatoes in the frying-pan with a baking-powder can, looking as fresh and rested as if she had been asleep all night, instead of holding a lonely vigil beside a stovepipe-hole.

John Corbett advanced to the table and solemnly deposited the green box thereon; then with painstaking deliberation he arranged the contents of his pockets in piles. Rance Belmont's watch lay by itself; then the bills according to denomination; last of all the silver and a slip of brown paper with writing on it in lead-pencil.

When all was complete, he nodded to Maggie to take charge of the proceedings.

Maggie hastily inspected the contents of the green box, and having satisfied herself that it was all there, she laid it up, high and dry, on the clock shelf.

Then she hastily looked at the piles and read the slip of brown paper, which seemed to stand for one sorrel pacer, one cutter, one set single harness, two goat robes.

"Rance," said Maggie, slowly, "we don't want a cent that don't belong to us. I put Da at playing with you in the hope he would win all away from you that you had, for we were bound to stop you from goin' away with that dear girl if it could be done, and we knew you couldn't go broke; but now you can't do any harm if you had all the money in the world, for she's just gone home a few minutes ago with her man."

Rance Belmont started forward with a smothered oath, which Mrs. Corbett ignored.

"So take your money and horse and all, Rance It ain't me and Da would keep a cent we haven't earned. Take it, Rance"—shoving it toward him—"there's no hard feelin's now, and good luck to you! Sure, I guess Da enjoyed the game, and it seems he hadn't forgot the way." Maggie Corbett could not keep a small note of triumph out of her voice.

Rance Belmont gathered up the money without a word, and, putting on his cap and overcoat, he left the Black Creek Stopping-House. John Corbett carried the green box upstairs and put it carefully back in its place of safety, while Maggie Corbett carefully peppered and salted the potatoes in the pan.

. . . .

When Robert Grant, of the Imperial Lumber Company, of Toronto, wakened from his slumber it was broad daylight, and the yellow winter sun poured in through the frosted panes. The events of the previous night came back to him by degrees; the sore place on his face reminding him of the slight difference of opinion between himself and his new friend, young Mr. Brown.

"Pretty nice, tasty room this young fellow has," he said to himself, looking around at the many evidences of daintiness and good taste.

"He's a dandy fine young fellow, that Brown. I could take to him without half trying."

Then he became conscious of low voices in the next room.

"Hello, Brown!" he called.

Fred appeared in the doorway with a smiling face.

"How do you feel this morning, Mr. Grant?" he asked.

"I feel hungry," Mr. Grant declared. "I want some more of your good prairie cooking. If I get another meal of it I believe I'll be able to make friends with my son-in-law. When are you going to let me get up?"

Just then there was a rustle of skirts and Evelyn came swiftly into the room.

"Oh, father! father!" she cried, kissing the old man over and over again. "You will forgive me, won't you?"

The old man's voice was husky with happy tears.

"I guess we won't talk about forgiveness, dearie—we're about even, I think—but we've had our lesson. I've got my girl back—and, Evelyn, I want you and Fred to come home with me for Christmas and forever. You've got the old man solid, Evelyn. I couldn't face a Christmas without you."

Evelyn kissed him again without speaking.

"I will apologize to your man, Evelyn," the

old man said, after a pause. " I haven't treated the boy right. I hope he won't hold it against me."

" Not a bit of it," declared Evelyn. " You don't know Fred—that's all."

" Oh, how did you get here, Evelyn? Do you live near here? I have been so glad to see you I forgot to ask."

" Mr. Brown brought me over," said Evelyn, unblushingly. " He came over early this morning to tell me you were here. Wasn't it nice of him?"

" He's a dandy fellow, this young Brown," said the old man, and then stopped abruptly.

Evelyn's eyes were sparkling with suppressed laughter.

" But where is Fred?" her father asked, with an effort, and Evelyn watched him girding himself for a painful duty.

" I'll call him," she said, sweetly.

The old man's grey eyes grew dark with excitement and surprise as his friend Brown came into the room and stood beside Evelyn and quite brazenly put his left arm around her waist. His face was a study in emotions as his quick brain grasped the situation. With a prolonged whistle he dropped back on the pillow, and pulling the counterpane over his face he shook with laughter.

"The joke is all on me," he cried. "I have been three or four different kinds of a fool."

Then he emerged from the bed-clothes and, sitting up, grasped Fred's outstretched hand.

"There's one thing, though, I am very proud of, Fred," he said; "I may not be a good judge of humanity myself, but I am glad to know that my girl had all her wits about her when she went to pick out a man for herself!"

.   .   .   .

Randolph and Reginald stayed in hiding until it was established beyond all doubt that their brother Fred was alive and well. Then they came back to the "Sailors' Rest," and life for them went on as before.

At Christmas time a bulky letter and a small white box came addressed to them, bearing the postmark of Bournemouth.

The brothers seized their letter with undiluted joy; it was addressed in a bold, masculine hand, a lawyer's undoubtedly—a striking though perhaps not conclusive proof that Aunt Patience had winged her flight.

They were a little bit disappointed that it had not black edges—they had always imagined that the "blow" would come with black edges.

Reginald opened it, read it, and let it fall to the floor.

Randolph opened it, read it, and let it fall to the floor.

It contained a thick announcement card, with heavy gold edge, and the news that it carried was to the effect that on December the first Miss Priscilla Abigail Patience Brydon had been united in marriage to Rev. Alfred William Henry Curtis Moreland, Rector of St. Albans, Tilbury-on-the-Stoke, and followed this with the information that Mr. and Mrs. Alfred William Henry Curtis Moreland would be at home after January the first in the Rectory, Appleblossom Court, Parklane Road, Tilbury-on-the-Stoke.

The envelope also contained a sweetly happy, fluttery little note from Aunt Patience, saying she hoped they were well, and that she would try to be a good mother to the Rector's four little boys.

The small white box contained two squares of wedding cake!

HE RUNAWAY GRANDMOTHER

The Runaway Grandmother

(Reprinted by permission of *The Globe*, Toronto.)

GEORGE SHAW came back to his desolate hearth, and, sitting by the untidy table, thought bitter things of women. The stove dripped ashes; the table overflowed with dirty dishes.

His last housekeeper had been gone a week— she had left by request. Incidentally there disappeared at the same time towels, pillow-covers, a few small tools, and many other articles which are of a size to go in a trunk.

His former housekeeper, second to the last, had been a teary-eyed English lady, who, as a child, had played with King George, and was well beloved by all the Royal family. She had a soul above work, and utterly despised Canadians. Once, when her employer remonstrated with her for wearing his best overcoat when she went to milk, she fell a-weeping and declared she wasn't going to be put on. Mr. Shaw said the same thing about his coat, and it led to unpleasantness. The next day he found her picking chips in his brown derby, and when he expressed his disapproval she told him it was no fit hat for a young man like him—he should have a topper. Mr. Shaw decided that he would try to do without her.

Before that he had had a red-cheeked Irishwoman, who cooked so well, scrubbed so industriously, that he had thought his troubles were all over. But one day she went to Millford, and came home in a state of wild exhilaration, with more of the same in a large black bottle. When Mr. Shaw came to put away the horse, she struck him over the head with her handbag, playfully blackening one of his eyes, and then begged him to come and make up—" kiss and forgit, like the swate pet that he was."

Exit Mrs. Murphy.

George Shaw decided to do his own cooking, but in three days every dish in the house was dirty; the teapot was full of leaves, the stove full of ashes, and the floor was slippery.

George Shaw's farm lay parallel with the Souris River in that fertile region which lies between the Brandon and the Tiger Hills. His fields ran an unbroken mile, facing the Tiger Hills, blue with mist. He was a successful young farmer, and he should have been a happy man without a care in the world, but he did not look it as he sat wearily by his red stove, with the deep furrows of care on his young face.

The busy time was coming on; he needed another man, and he did hate trying to do the cooking himself.

As a last hope he decided to advertise. He hunted up his writing-pad and wrote hastily:

"Housekeeper wanted by a farmer; must be sober and steady. Good wages to the right person. Apply to George Shaw, Millford, Man."

He read it over reflectively. "There ought to be someone for me," he said. "I am not hard to please. Any good, steady old lady who will give me a bite to eat, not swear at me or wear my clothes or drink while on duty will answer my purpose."

Two days after his advertisement had appeared in the Brandon *Times*, "she" arrived.

Shaw saw a smart-looking woman gaily tripping along the road, and his heart failed.

As she drew near, however, he was relieved to find that her hair was snowy white.

"Good evening, Mr. Shaw!" she called to him as soon as she was within speaking distance.

"Good evening, madam," he replied, lifting his hat.

"I just asked along the road until I found you," she said, untying her bonnet strings; "I knew this lonesome little house must be the place. No trees, no flowers, no curtains, no washing on the line—I could tell there was no woman around." She was fixing her hair at his little glass as she spoke. " Now, son, run out and get a few chips for the fire, and we'll have a bite of supper in a few minutes."

Shaw brought the chips.

" Now, what do you say to pancakes for supper?"

Shaw declared that nothing would suit him so well as pancakes.

The fire crackled merrily under the kettle, and soon the two of them were sitting down to an appetizing meal of pancakes and syrup, boiled eggs and tea.

" Land sakes, George, you must have had your own time with those housekeepers of yours! Some of them drank, eh? I could tell that by the piece you put in the paper. But never mind them now; I'll soon have you feeling fine as silk. How's your socks? Toes out, I'll bet. Well, I'll hunt you up a pair, if there's any to be found. If I can't find any you can go to bed when you get your chores done, and I'll wash out them you've on—I can't bear my men folks to have their toes out; a hole in the heel ain't so bad, it's behind you and you can forget it, but a hole in the toe is always in your way no matter which way you're going."

After supper, when Shaw was out doing his chores, he could see her bustling in and out of the house; now she was beating his bedclothes on the line; in another minute she was leaning far out of a bedroom window dusting a pillow.

When he came into the house she reported that her search for stockings, though vigorous, had been vain. He protested a little about having to go to bed when the sun was shining, but she insisted.

"I'm sorry, George," she said, "to have to make you go to bed, but it's the only thing we can do. You'll find your bed feels a lot better since I took the horse collar and the pair of rubber boots out from under the mattress. That's a poor place to keep things. Good-night now—don't read lying down."

When he went upstairs Shaw noticed with dismay that his lamp had gone from the box beside his bed. So he was not likely to disobey her last injunction—at least, not for any length of time.

Just at daylight the next morning there came a knock at his door.

"Come, George—time to get up!"

When he came in from feeding his horses a splendid breakfast was on the table.

"Here's your basin, George; go out and have a good wash. Here's your comb; it's been lost for quite awhile. I put a towel out there for you, too. Hurry up now and get your vittles while they are nice!"

When Shaw came to the table she regarded him with pleasure.

"You're a fine-looking boy, George, when you're slicked up," she said. "Now bow your head until we say grace! There, now pitch in and tell me how you like grandma's cooking."

Shaw ate heartily and praised everything.

A few days afterwards she said, "Now, George, I guess I'll have to ask you to go to town and get some things we need for the house."

Shaw readily agreed, and took out his paper and pencil.

"Soap, starch, ten yards of cheesecloth—that's for curtains," she said. "I'll knit lace for them, and they'll look real dressy; toilet soap, sponge and nailbrush—that's for your bath, George; you haven't been taking them as often as you should, or the hoops wouldn't have come off your tub. You can't cheat Nature, George; she always tells on you. Ten yards flannelette—that's for night-shirts; ten yards sheeting—that's for your bed—and your white shirts are pretty far gone."

"How do you know?" he asked in surprise; "they are all in my trunk."

"Yes, I know, and the key is in that old cup on the stand, and I know how to unlock a trunk, don't I?" she replied with dignity. "You need new shirts all right, but just get one. I never could abear them boughten shirts, they are so skimpy in the skirt; I'll make you some lovely ones, with blue and pink flossin' down the front."

He looked up alarmed.

"Then about collars," she went on serenely. "You have three, but they're not in very good shape, though, of course, you couldn't expect anything better of them, kept in that box with the nails—oh, I found them, George, you needn't look so surprised. You see I know something about boys—I have three of my own." A shadow passed over her face and she sighed. "Well, I guess that is all for to-day. Be sure to get your mail and hurry home."

"Shall I tell the postmaster to put your mail in my box?" he asked.

"Oh, no, never mind—I ain't expectin' any," she said, and Shaw drove away wondering.

A few nights after she said, "Well, George, I suppose you are wonderin' now who this old lady is, though I am not to say real old either."

"Indeed you are not old," Shaw declared with considerable gallantry; "you are just in your prime."

She regarded him gratefully. "You're a real nice boy, George," she said, "and there ain't going to be no secrets between us. If you wet your feet, or tear your clothes, don't try to hide it. Don't keep nothing from me and I won't keep nothing from you. Now I'll tell you who I am and all about it. I am Mrs. Peter Harris, of Owen Sound, Ontario, and I have three sons here in the West. They've all done well, fur as money goes. I came up to visit them. I came from Bert's here. I couldn't stand the way Bert's folks live. Mind you, they burn their lights all night, and they told me it doesn't cost a cent more. Land o' liberty! They can't fool me. If lights burn, someone pays—and the amount of hired help they keep is something scandalous. Et, that is Bert's wife, is real smart, and they have two hired girls, besides their own two girls, and they get in a woman to wash besides. I wanted them to let the two girls go while I was there, but no, sir! Et says, ' Grandma, you didn't come here to work, you must just rest.' They wouldn't let me do a thing, and that brazen hired girl—the housemaid, they call her—one day even made my bed; and, mind you, George, she put the narrow hem on the sheet to the top, and she wasn't a bit ashamed when I told her. She said she hoped it didn't make me feel that I was standin' on my head all night; and the way that woman hung out the clothes was a perfect scandal!" Her voice fell to an awed whisper. " She hangs the underwear in plain sight. I ain't never been used to the like of that! I could not stay. Bert is kind enough, so is Et, and they have one girl, Maud, that I really do like. She is twenty-one, but, of course, brought up the way she has been, she is awful ignorant for that age. Mind you, that girl had never turned the heel of a stocking until I got her at it, but Maud can learn. I'd take that girl quick, and bring her up like my own, if Bert would let me. Well, anyway, I could not put up with the way they live, and I just ran away."

"You ran away!" echoed Shaw. "They'll be looking for you!"

"Let 'em look!" said the old lady, grimly. "They won't ever find me here."

"I'll hide you in the haymow, and if they come in here to search for you I'll declare I never knew you—I am prepared to do desperate things," Shaw declared.

"George, if they ever get in here—that is, Et anyway—she'll know who did the fixin' up. There ain't many that know how to do this Rocky Road to Dublin that is on your lounge. Et would know who'd been here."

"That settles it!" declared Shaw. "Et shall not enter. If Et gets in it shall be over my prostrate form, but maybe it would be better for you to take the Rocky Road with you to the hayloft!"

The old lady laughed heartily. "Ain't we happy, George, you and me? I've tried all my own, and they won't let me have one bit of my own way. Out at Edward's—he's a lawyer at Regina—I tried to get them all to go to bed at half-past ten—late enough, too, for decent people —and didn't Edward's wife get real miffed over it? And then I went to Tom's—he's a doctor

down at Winnipeg, but he's all gone to politics;
he was out night after night makin' speeches,
and he had a young fellow lookin' after his prac-
tice who wouldn't know a corn from a gumboil
only they grow in different places. Tom's pa
and me spent good money on his education, and
it's hard for us to see him makin' no use of it
He was nice enough to me, wanted me to stay
and be company for Edith, but I told him he
should try to be company for Edith himself.
Well, he didn't get elected—that's one comfort.
I believe it was an answer to prayer. Maybe
he'll settle down to his doctorin' now. Then I
went to Bert's, and I soon saw I could not stay
there. Just as soon as I saw your little bit in
the paper, I says, ' The Lord has opened a door!'
I gave Maud a hint that I would clear out some
day and go where I would be let work, and the
dear child says to me, ' Grandma, if I ever get
a house of my own you can come and live with
me, and you can do every bit of the work, and
everyone will have to do just what you say;
they'll have to go to bed at sundown if you say
so.' Maud's the best one I have belongin' to me.
She'll give them a hint that I'm all right."

But Shaw was apprehensive. He knew who
Bert was, and he had uncomfortable visions of
Mr. Albert Harris driving up to his door some
day and demanding that Mrs. Peter Harris, his
mother, immediately come home with him; and

the fear and dread of former housekeepers swept over George Shaw's soul. No, he would not give her up! Of course, there were times when he thought she was rather exacting, and when he felt some sympathy for Edward's wife for getting " miffed."

When she was with him about a week she announced that he must have a daily bath! " It is easier to wash you than the bed-clothes, that's one reason," she said, " and it's good for you besides. That's what's wrong with lots of young boys; they git careless and dirty, and then they take to smoking and drinking just natcherally A clean hide, mind you, is next to a clean heart Now go along upstairs; everything is ready for you."

Henceforth there was no danger of the hoops falling off the tub, for it was in daily use, and, indeed, it was not many nights until George Shaw looked forward with pleasure to his nightly wash.

The old lady's face glowed with pleasure as she went about her work, or sat sewing in the shade of the house. At her instigation Shaw had put up a shed for his machinery, which formerly had littered the yard, and put his wood in even piles.

The ground fell away in a steep ravine, just in front of the house, and pink wild roses and columbine hung in profusion over the spring which gushed out of the bank. Away to the east were the sand-hills of the Assiniboine—the bad lands of the prairie, their surface peopled with stiff spruce trees that stand like sentries looking, always looking out across the plain!

Mrs. Harris often sat with her work in the shade of the house, on pleasant afternoons, looking at this peaceful scene, and her heart was full of gladness and content.

The summer passed pleasantly for George Shaw and his cheery old housekeeper. Not a word did they hear from " Bert's " folks.

"I would like to see Maud," Mrs. Harris said one night to Shaw as she sat knitting a sock for him beside their cheerful fireside. He was reading.

"What is Maud like?" he asked.

"Maud favors my side of the house," she answered. "She's a pretty good-looking girl, very much the hi'th and complexion I used to be when I was her age. You'd like Maud fine if you saw her, George."

"I don't want to see her," Shaw replied, "for I am afraid that the coming of Maud might mean the departure of Grandma, and that would be a bad day for me."

"I ain't goin' to leave you, George, and I believe Maud would be reasonable if she did come! She'd see how happy we are!"

THE RUNAWAY GRANDMOTHER

It was in the early autumn that Maud came. The grain had all been cut and stacked, and was waiting for the thresher to come on its rounds. Shaw was ploughing in the field in front of his house when Maud came walking briskly up the road just as her grandmother had done four months before! The trees in the poplar grove beside the road were turning red and yellow with autumn, and Maud, in her red-brown suit and hat, looked as if she belonged to the picture.

Some such thought as this struggled in Shaw's brain and shone in his eyes as he waited for her at the headland.

He raised his hat as she drew near. Maud went right into the subject.

"Have you my grandmother?" she asked.

Shaw hesitated—the dreaded moment had come. Visions of former housekeepers—dirty dishes, unmade bed, dust, flies, mice—rose before him and tempted him to say "no," but something stronger and better, perhaps it was the "clean hide" prompting the clean heart, spoke up in him.

"I have your grandmother," he said slowly, "and she is very well and happy."

"Will you give her up?" was Maud's next question.

"Never!" he answered stoutly; "and she won't give me up, either. Your grandmother and I are very fond of each other, I would like you to know—but come in and see her."

That night after supper, which proved to be a very merry meal in spite of the shadow which had fallen across the little home, Mrs. Harris said almost tearfully: "I can't leave this pore lamb, Maud—there's no knowin' what will happen to him."

"I will go straight back to the blanket and dog soup," Shaw declared with cheerful conviction. "You can't imagine the state things were in when your grandmother came—bed not made since Christmas, horsenails for buttons, comb and brush lost but not missed, wash basin rusty! Your grandmother, of course, has been severe with me—she makes me go to bed before sundown. Yet I refuse to part with her. Who takes your grandmother takes me; and now, Miss Maud, it is your move!"

That night when they sat in the small sitting-room with a bright fire burning in the shining stove, Maud felt her claim on her grandmother growing more and more shadowy. Mrs. Harris was in a radiant humor. She was knitting lace for the curtains, and chatted gaily as she worked.

"You see, Maud, I am never lonely here; it's a real heartsome place to live. There's the trains goin' by twice a day, and George here is a real good hand to read out to me. We're not

near done with the book we're reading, and I
am anxious to see if Adam got the girl. He was
set on havin' her, but some of her folks were in
for makin' trouble."

"Folks sometimes do!" said Shaw, meaningly

"Well, I can't go until we finish the book,"
the old lady declared, "and we see how the
story comes out, and I don't believe Maud is
the one to ask it."

Maud made a pretty picture as she sat with
one shapely foot on the fender of the stove, the
firelight dancing on her face and hair. Shaw,
looking at her, forgot the errand on which she
came—forgot everything only that she was
there.

"Light the lamp and read a bit of the book
now," Mrs. Harris said. "Maud'll like it, I
know. She's the greatest girl for books!"

Shaw began to read. It was "The Kentucky
Cardinal" he read, that exquisite love-story,
that makes us lovers all, even if we never have
been, or worse still, have forgotten. Shaw loved
the book, and read it tenderly, and Maud, leaning back in her chair, found her heart warmed
with a sudden great content.

A week later Shaw and Maud walked along
the river bank and discussed the situation
Autumn leaves carpeted the ground beneath
their feet, and the faint murmur of the river be
low as it slipped over its pebbly bed came faintly

to their ears. In the sky above them, wild geese with flashing white wings honked away toward the south, and a meadow lark, that jolly fellow who comes early and stays late, on a red-leafed haw-tree poured out his little heart in melody.

"You see, Mr. Shaw," Maud was saying, "it doesn't look right for Grandma to be living with a stranger when she has so many of her own people. I know she is happy with you—happier than she has been with any of us—but what will people think? It looks as if we didn't care for her, and we do. She is the sweetest old lady in the world." Maud was very much in earnest.

Shaw's eyes followed the wild geese until they faded into tiny specks on the horizon. Then he turned and looked straight into her face.

"Maud," he said, with a strange vibration in his voice, " I know a way out of the difficulty; a real good, pleasant way, and by it your grandmother can continue to live with me, and still be with her own folks. Maud, can you guess it?"

The blush that spread over Maud's face indicated that she was a good guesser!

Then the meadow-lark, all unnoticed, hopped a little nearer, and sang sweeter than ever. Not that anybody was listening, either!

THE RETURN TICKET

The Return Ticket

(Reprinted by permission of *The Canadian Ladies'*
Home Journal.)

IN the station at Emerson, the boundary town,
we were waiting for the Soo train, which comes
at an early hour in the morning. It was a bitterly cold, dark, winter morning; the wires overhead sang dismally in the wind, and even the
cheer of the big coal fire that glowed in the rusty
stove was dampened by the incessant mourning
of the storm.

Along the walls, on the benches, sat the track-
men, in their sheepskin coats and fur caps, with
earlaps tied tightly down. They were tired and
sleepy, and sat in every conceivable attitude ex-
pressive of sleepiness and fatigue. A red lantern, like an evil eye, gleamed from one dark corner; in the middle of the floor were several green
lamps turned low, and over against the wall
hung one barred lantern whose bright little
gleam of light reminded one uncomfortably of a
small, live mouse in a cage, caught and doomed,
but undaunted still. The telegraph instruments
clicked at intervals. Two men, wrapped in over-

131

coats, stood beside the stove and talked in low tones about the way real estate was increasing in value in Winnipeg.

The door opened and a big fellow, another snow shoveller, came in hurriedly, letting in a burst of flying snow that sizzled on the hot stove. It did not rouse the sleepers from the bench; neither did the new-comer's remark that it was a "deuce of a night" bring forth any argument —we were one on that point.

The train was late; the night agent told us that when he came out to shovel in more coal— "she" was delayed by the storm.

I leaned back and tried to be comfortable. After all, I thought, it might easily be worse. I was going home after a pleasant visit. I had many agreeable things to think of, and still I kept thinking to myself that it was not a cheerful night. The clock, of course, indicated that it was morning, but the deep black that looked in through the frosted windows, the heavy shadows in the room, which the flickering lanterns only seemed to emphasize, were all of the night, and bore no relation to the morning.

The train came at last with a roar that drowned the voice of the storm. The sleepers on the bench sprang up like one man, seized their lanterns, and we all rushed out together. The long coach that I entered was filled with tired, sleepy-looking people, who had been sitting up all night. They were curled up uncomfortably, making a brave attempt to rest, all except one little old lady, who sat upright, looking out into the black night. When the official came to ask the passengers where they were going, I heard her tell him that she was a Canadian, and she had been " down in the States with Annie, and now she was bringing Annie home," and as she said this she pointed significantly ahead to the baggage car.

There was something about the old lady that appealed to me. I went over to her when the official had gone out. No, she wasn't tired, she said; she " had been up a good many nights, and been worried some, but the night before last she had had a real good sleep."

She was quite willing to talk; the long black night had made her glad of companionship.

" I took Annie to Rochester, down in Minnesota, to see the doctors there—the Mayos—did you ever hear of the Mayos? Well, Dr. Smale, at Rose Valley, said they were her only hope. Annie had been ailing for years, and Dr. Smale had done all he could for her. Dr. Moore, our old doctor, wouldn't hear of it; he said an operation would kill her, but Annie was set on going. I heard Annie say to him that she'd rather die than live sick, and she would go to Rochester. Dave Johnston—Annie's man, that is—he drinks, you know—"

133

THE RETURN TICKET

The old lady's voice fell and her tired old face seemed to take on deeper lines of trouble as she sat silent with her own sad thoughts. I expressed my sorrow.

"Yes, Annie had her own troubles, poor girl," she said at last; "and she was a good girl, Annie was, and she deserved something better. She was a tender-hearted girl, and gentle and quiet, and never talked back to anyone, to Dave least of all, for she worshipped the very ground he walked on, and married him against all our wishes. She thought she could reform him!"

She said it sadly, but without bitterness.

"Was he good to her?" I asked. People draw near together in the stormy dark of a winter's morning, and the thought of Annie in her narrow box ahead robbed my question of any rudeness.

"He was good to her in his own way," Annie's mother said, trying to be quite just, "but it was a rough way. She had a fine, big, brick house to live in—it was a grand house, but it was a lonely house. He often went away and stayed for weeks, and her not knowing where he was or how he would come home. He worried her always. The doctor said that was part of her trouble—he worried her too much."

"Did he ever try to stop drinking?" I asked. I wanted to think better of him if I could.

" Yes, he did; he was sober once for nearly a
year, and Annie's health was better than it had
been for years, but the crowd around the hotel
there in Rose Valley got after him every chance,
and one Christmas Day they got him going again.
Annie never could bear to mention about him
drinkin' to anyone, not even me—it would ha'
been easier on her if she could ha' talked about
it, but she wasn't one of the talkin' kind."

We sat in silence, listening to the pounding of
the rails.

" Everybody was kind to her in Rochester,"
she said, after a while. " When we were sitting
there waitin' our turn—you know how the sick
people wait there in two long rows, waitin' to be
taken in to the consultin' room, don't you? Well,
when we were sittin' there Annie was sufferin'
pretty bad, and we were still a long way from
the top of the line. Dr. Judd was takin' them
off as fast as he could, and the ambulances were
drivin' off every few minutes, takin' them away
to the hospital after the doctors had decided
what was wrong with them. Some of them didn't
need to go to the hospital at all—they're the
best off, I think. We got talkin' to the people
around us—they are there from all over the
country, with all kinds of diseases, poor people.
Well, there was a man from Kansas City who
had been waitin' a week, but had got up now
second to the end, and I noticed him lookin' at

Annie. I was fannin' her and tryin' to keep her cheered up. Her face was a bad color from the pain she was in, and what did this man do but git up and come down to us and tell Annie that she could have his place. He said he wasn't in very bad pain now, and he would take her place. He made very little of it, but it meant a lot to us, and to him, too, poor fellow. Annie didn't want to do it, but he insisted. Sick folks know how to be kind to sick folks, I tell you."

The dawn began to show blue behind the frost ferns on the window and the lamps overhead looked pale and sickly in the grey light.

"Annie had her operation on Monday," she went on after a long pause. "She was lookin' every day for a letter from Dave, and when the doctor told her they would operate on her on Monday morning early, she asked him if he would mind putting it off until noon. She thought there would be a letter from Dave, for sure, on that morning's mail. The doctor was very kind to her—they understand a lot, them Mayos—and he did put it off. In the ward with Annie there was a little woman from Saskatche-wan, that was a very bad case. She talked to us a lot about her man and her four children. She had a real good man by what she said. They were on a homestead near Quill Lake, and she was so sure she'd get well. The doctor was very hope-

ful of Annie, and said she had nine chances out
of ten of getting better, but this little woman's
was a worse case. Dr. Will Mayo told her she
had just one chance in ten—but, dear me, she
was a brave woman; she spoke right up quick,
and says she, 'That's all I want; I'll get well if
I've only half a chance. I've got to; Jim and
the children can't do without me.' Jim was her
man. When they came to take her out into the
operating room they couldn't give her ether,
some way. She grabbed the doctor's hand, and
says she, kind of chokin' up, all at once, 'You'll
do your best for Jim's sake, won't you?' and he
says, says he, 'My dear woman, I'll do my best
for your sake.' Busy and all as they are, they're
the kindest men in the world, and just before
they began to operate the nurse brought her a
letter from Jim and read it to her, and she held
it in her hand through it all, and when they
wheeled her back into the ward after the operation, it was still in her hand, though she had
fainted dead away."

"Did Annie get her letter?" I asked her.

My companion did not answer at once, but I
knew very well that the letter had not come.

"She didn't ask for it at the last; she just
looked at me before they put the gauze thing over
her face. I knew what she meant. I had been
down to see if it had come, and they told me all

the mails were in for the day from the West. She just looked at me so pitiful, but it was like Annie not to ask. A letter from Dave would have comforted her so, but it didn't come, though I wired him two days before telling him when the operation would be. Annie was wonderful cheerful and calm, but I was trembling like a leaf when they were givin' her the ether, and when they wheeled her out all so stiff and white I just seemed to feel I'd lost my girl."

I took the old lady's hand and tried to whisper words of comfort. She returned the pressure of my hand; her eyes were tearless, and her voice did not even waver, but the thought of poor Annie going into the valley unassured by any loving word gave free passage to my tears.

"Did Dave write or wire?" I asked when I could speak.

"No, not a word; he's likely off on a spree." The old lady spoke bitterly now. "Everybody was kind to my Annie but him, and it was a word from him that would have cheered her the most. Dr. Mayo came and sat beside her just an hour before she died, and says he, 'You still have a chance, Mrs. Johnston,' but Annie just thanked him again for his kindness and sort o' shook her head. . . . .

"The little woman from Saskatchewan didn't do well at all after the operation, and Dr. Mayo

138

was afraid she wouldn't pull through. She asked him what chance she had, and he told her straight—the Mayos always tell the truth—that she had only one chance in a hundred. She was so weak that he had to bend down to hear her whisperin', 'I'll take that one chance!'"

"And did she?" I asked eagerly.

"She was still living when I left. She will get better, I think. She has a very good man, by what she was tellin' us, and a woman can stand a lot if she has a good man," the old lady said, with the wisdom born of experience. "I've nursed around a lot, and I've always noticed that!"

I have noticed it, too, though I've never "nursed around."

"Dave came with us to the station the day we left home. He was sober that day, and gave Annie plenty of money. Annie told him to get a return ticket for her, too. I said he'd better get just a single for her, for she might have to stay longer than a month; but she said no, she'd be back in a month, all right. Dave seemed pleased to hear her talk so cheerful. When she got her ticket she sat lookin' at it a long time. I knew what she was thinkin'. She never was a girl to talk mournful, and when the conductor tore off the goin' down part she gave me the return piece, and she says, 'You take this, mother.' I knew that she was thinkin' what the return half might be used for."

We changed cars at Newton, and I stood with the old lady and watched the trainmen unload the long box. They threw off trunks, boxes and valises almost viciously, but when they lifted up the long box their manner changed and they laid it down as tenderly as if they had known something of Annie and her troubled life.

We sent another telegram to Dave, and then sat down in the waiting-room to wait for the west train. The wind drove the snow in billows over the prairie, and the early twilight of the morning was bitterly cold.

Her train came first, and again the long box was gently put aboard. On the wind-swept platform Annie's mother and I shook hands without a word, and in another minute the long train was sweeping swiftly across the white prairie. I watched it idly, thinking of Annie and her sad home-going. Just then the first pale beams of the morning sun glinted on the last coach, and touched with fine gold the long white smoke plume, which the wind carried far over the field. There is nothing so cheerful as the sunshine, and as I sat in the little grey waiting-room, watching the narrow golden beam that danced over the closed wicket, I could well believe that a rest remains for Annie, and that she is sure of a welcome at her journey's end. And as the sun's warmth began to thaw the tracery of frost on the window, I began to hope that God's grace may yet find out Dave, and that he too may "make good" in the years to come. As for the little woman from Quill Lake, who was still willing to take the one chance, I have never had the slightest doubt.

THE UNGRATEFUL PIGEONS

The Ungrateful Pigeons

(Reprinted by permission of *The Canadian Home Journal*.)

PHILIP was a little boy, with a generous growth of freckles, and a loving heart. Most people saw only the freckles, but his mother never lost sight of his affectionate nature. So when, one warm spring day, he sat moodily around the house, she was ready to listen to his grievance.

" I want something for a pet," said Philip. " I have no dog or cat or anything!"

" What would you like the very best of all?" his mother asked, with the air of a fairy god-mother.

" I want pigeons! They are so pretty and white and soft, and they lay eggs and hatch young ones."

All his gloom had vanished!

" How much a pair?" asked his mother.

" Twenty-five cents out at Crane's. They have millions of them; I can walk out—it's only five miles."

" Where will we put them when you bring them home?" she asked.

THE UNGRATEFUL PIGEONS

Philip thought they could share his room, but this suggestion was promptly rejected!

Then Philip's father was hurriedly interviewed by Philip's mother, and he agreed to nail a box on the end of the stable, far beyond the reach of prowling cats, and Philip, armed with twenty-five cents, set forth gaily on his five-mile walk. It was Saturday morning, and a beautiful day of glittering April sunshine. The sun was nearly down when Philip returned, tired but happy. It seemed there had been some trouble in catching them. The quoted price of twenty-five cents a pair was for raw, uncaught pigeons, but Philip had succeeded at last and brought back two beauties, one with blue markings, and the other one almost white.

The path of true love never ran smooth; difficulties were encountered at once. Philip put a generous supply of straw in one end of the box for a bed, but when he put them in they turned round and round as if they were not quite satisfied with their lodgings. Then Philip had one of those dazzling ideas which so often led to trouble with the other members of his family. He made a hurried visit to Rose's—his sister's—room. Rose was a grown-up lady of twelve.

When he came back, he brought with him a dove-grey chiffon auto veil, the kind that was much favored that spring by young ladies in Rose's set, for a head protection instead of hats.

146

THE UNGRATEFUL PIGEONS

Rose's intimate friend, Hattie Matthews, had that very day put a knot in each side, which made it fit very artistically on Rose's head. Philip carefully untied the knots, and draped it over the straw. The effect was beautiful. Philip exclaimed with delight! They looked so pretty and " woozy "!

In the innocence of his heart, he ran into the house, for Rose; he wanted her to rejoice with him.

Rose's language was pointed, though dignified, and the pretty sight was ruthlessly broken up. Philip's mother, however, stepped into the gap, and produced an old, pale blue veil of her own, which was equally becoming.

It was she, too, who proposed a pigeon book, and a very pleasant time was spent making it,— for it was not a common book, bought with money, but one made by loving hands. Several sheets of linen notepaper were used for the inside, with stiff yellow paper for the cover, the whole fastened with pale blue silk. Then Philip printed on the cover:

Philip Brown,
Pigeon Book,

but not in any ordinary, plain, little bits of letters! Each capital was topped off with an arrow, and ended with a feather, and even the small letters had a thick blanket of dots.

THE UNGRATEFUL PIGEONS

The first entry was as follows:

April 7th.—*I wocked out to Crane's, and got 2 fantales. they are hard to ketch. I payed 25 scents. My father knailed a box on the stable, and I put in a bed of straw, they are bootiful. my sister would not let me have her vale, but I got one prettier. they look woozy.*

The next day, Sunday, Philip did not see how he could go to church or Sunday-school—he had not time, he said, but his mother agreed to watch the pigeons, and so his religious obligations did not need to be set aside.

Monday afternoon the Browns' back yard was full of little boys inspecting Philip's pigeons, not merely idle onlookers, but hard-headed poultry fanciers, as shown by the following entry:

April 9th.—*I sold a pare of white ones to-day to Wilfred Garbett, to be kept three weeks after birth, Eva Gayton wants a pare too any color, in July. She paid for them.*

Under this entry, which was made laboriously in ink, there was another one, in lead pencil, done by Philip's brother, Jack:

This is called selling Pigeons short.

Philip's friends recommended many and varied things for the pigeons to eat, and he did his best to supply them all, as far as his slender

148

means allowed; he went to the elevator for
wheat; he traded his good jack-knife for two
mouse-eaten and anæmic heads of squaw-corn,
which were highly recommended by an unscru-
pulous young Shylock, who had just come to
town and was short of a jack-knife. His handkerchief, scribblers and pencils mysteriously disappeared, but other articles came in their place:
a small round mirror advertising corsets on the
back (Gordon Smith said pigeons liked a looking-glass—it made them more contented to stay
at home) ; a small swing out of a birdcage, which
was duly put in place (vendor Miss Edie Beal,
owner unknown). Of course, it was too small
for pigeons, but there were going to be little
ones very soon, weren't there?

He also brought to them one day five sun-
flower seeds, recommended and sold by a mild-
eyed little Murphy girl, who had the stubby fingers of a money-maker. Philip, being very low
in funds that day, wanted her to accept pros-
pective eggs in payment, but the stubby-fingered
Miss Murphy preferred currency! Philip decided to make no entry of these transactions in
his Pigeon Book.

His young brother, Barrie, began to be troublesome about this time, and to evince an un-
wholesome interest in the pigeons. The ladder,
which was placed against the stable under their
house, at first seemed to him too high to climb,

but seeing the multitude of delighted spectators
who went up and down without accident, he
resolved to try it, too, and so successfully that
he was able after a few attempts to carry a stick
with him, stand on the highest rung, and poke up
the pigeons.

One day he was caught—with the goods—by
Philip himself. So indignant was Philip that
for a moment he stood speechless. His young
brother, jarred by a guilty conscience and fear
of Philip, came hastily down the ladder, raising
a few bruises on his anatomy as he came. Even
in his infant soul he felt he deserved all he had
got, and thought best not to mention the occur-
rence. Philip, too, generously kept quiet about
it, feeling that the claims of justice had been met.
The only dissatisfied parties in the transaction
were the pigeons.

The next Sunday in Sabbath School there was
a temperance lesson, and Barrie Brown quoted
the Golden Text with a slight variation—"At
the last it biteth like a serpent and stingeth like
a *ladder!*"

Philip was the only one who knew what he
meant, and he said it served him good and right.

The following entry appears in the Pigeon
Book:

*My brother Barrie poks them, but he got his
leson. tomoro I'll let them out—there fond
enough of home now I gess.*

THE UNGRATEFUL PIGEONS

The next day being Saturday, when Philip could watch them, he let them out. All day long his heart was torn with pride and fear—they looked so beautiful, circling and wheeling over the stable and far away across the road, and yet his heart was chill with the fear that they would never return.

That night the Pigeon Book received the following entry:

April 21st.—I let them out and they came back —they are sweet pets. I dreem about them every night   I have two dreems, my good dreem is the've layd my bad dreem is about tomcats and two little heaps of fethers its horrid.

The next week another entry went into the book:

I sold another pare to-day I've razed the price this pare is to be delivered in Ogist. I gave them a bran mash to-day, it makes them lay sure.

Under this Jack wrote:

Thinking of the August delivery.

The next entry was this:

May 1st.—Wilfred G. is pritty meen, he thinks he knows it all. they aint goin to lay all in a hurry.

THE UNGRATEFUL PIGEONS

There seemed to be no doubt about this. They certainly were not. In spite of bran mashes, pepper, cotton batting, blue veil and tender care, they refused to even consider the question of laying.

Philip was quite satisfied with them as they were, if they would only stay with him, but the customers who had bought and paid for highly recommended young fowl were inclined to be impatient and even unpleasant when the two parent birds were to be seen gadding around the street at all hours of the day, utterly regardless of their young master's promises.

Philip learned to call them. His "cutacutacoo—cutacutacoo" could be heard up and down the street. Sometimes they seemed to pay a little attention to him, and then his joy was full. More often they seemed to say, "Cutacutacoo yourself!" or some such saucy word, and fly farther away.

One night they did not come home. Philip's most insistent "cutacutacoo" brought no response. He hired boys to help him to look for them, beggaring himself of allies and marbles, even giving away his Lucky Shooter, a mottled pee-wee, to a lynx-eyed young hunter who claimed to be able to see in the dark. He even dared the town constable by staying out long after the curfew had rung, looking and asking No one had seen them.

THE UNGRATEFUL PIGEONS

Through the night it rained, a cold, cruel rain
—or so it seemed to the sad-hearted, wide-awake
little boy. He stole out quietly, afraid that he
might be sent back to bed, but only his mother
heard him, and she understood. It was lonesome and dark outside, but love lighted his way.
He groped his way up the ladder, hoping to find
them, but though the straw, the cotton batting,
the blue veil, the water-dish were all in place—
there were no pigeons!

Philip came back to bed, cold and wet in body,
but his heart colder still with fear, and his face
wetter with tears. Under cover of the night a
boy of ten can cry all he wants to.

His mother, who heard him going out and
who understood, called softly to him to come to
her room, and then sympathized. She said they
were safe enough, never fear, with some flock of
pigeons; they had got lonesome, that was all;
they would come back when they got hungry,
and the rain would not hurt them, and be sure
to wipe his feet!

The next day they were found across the street
with Jerry Andrews' pigeons, as unconcerned as
you please. Philip parted with his Lost Heir
game—about the only thing he had left—to get
Jerry to help him to catch them when they were
roosting. He shut them up for a few days and
worked harder than ever, if that were possible,
to try to please them.

THE UNGRATEFUL PIGEONS

The Pigeon Book would have been neglected only for his mother, who said it was only right to put in the bad as well as the good. That was the way with all stories. Philip made this entry:

They went away and staid and had to be brot back by force   I guess they were lonesome.   I don't know why they don't like me—I like them!

When his mother read that she said, " Poor little fellow," and made pancakes for tea.

In a few days he let them out again, and watched them with a pale face.

They did not hesitate a minute, but flew straight away down the street to the place they had been before, to the place where the people often made pies of pigeons and were not ashamed to tell it!

Philip followed them silently, not having the heart to call.

" Say, Phil," the boy of the pigeon loft called —he was a stout boy who made money out of everything—" I guess they ain't goin' to stay with you. You might as well sell out to me. I'll give you ten cents for the pair. I'm goin' to sell a bunch to the hotel on Saturday."

An insane desire to fight him took hold of Philip. He turned away without speaking.

At school that day he approached the pigeon boy and made the proposition that filled the boy with astonishment: " I'll give them to you, Jerry," he said, hurriedly, " if you promise not to kill them. It's all right! I guess I won't bother with pigeons—I think I'll get a dog—or something," he ended lamely.

Jerry was surprised, but being a business man he closed the deal on the spot. When Philip went home he put his pigeon book away.

There was a final entry, slightly smeared and very badly written:

They are ungrateful broots!

YOU NEVER CAN TELL

ز

You Never Can Tell

(Reprinted by permission of *Saturday Night*, Toronto.)

IT was at exactly half-past three in the afternoon of a hot June day that Mrs. Theodore Banks became smitten with the idea. Mrs. Banks often said afterwards she did not know how she came to be thinking about the Convention of the Arts and Crafts at all, although she is the Secretary. The idea was so compelling that Mrs. Banks rushed down town to tell Mr. Banks—she felt she could not depend on the telephone.

"Ted," she cried, when she opened the door of the office, "I have an idea!"

Theodore raised his eyelids.

Mrs. Banks was flushed and excited and looked well. Mrs. Banks was a handsome woman any time, and to-day her vivacity was quite genuine.

"You know the Convention of the Arts and Crafts—which begins on the twentieth."

"I've heard of it—somewhere."

"Well, it just came to me, Teddy, what a perfectly heavenly thing it would be to invite that little Mrs. Dawson, who writes reviews for one of the papers here—you remember I told you about her—she is awfully clever and artistic and good-looking, and lives away off from every place, and her husband is not her equal at all— perfectly illiterate, I heard—uncultured anyway. What a perfect joy it would be to her to have her come, and meet with people who are her equals. She's an Ottawa girl originally, I believe, and she does write the most perfectly sweet and darling things—you remember I've read them for you. Of course, she is probably very shabby and out of date in her clothes by this time. But it doesn't really matter what one wears, if one has heaps of brains. It is only dull women, really, who have to be so terribly careful about what they wear, and spend so much money that way!"

"Dull women!" Theodore murmured. "Oh! is that why? I never really knew."

She laughed at his look of enlightened surprise. When Mrs. Banks laughed there were three dimples plainly showing, which did not entirely discourage her merriment.

"And you know, Teddy, there is such a mystery about her marriage! She will really be quite an acquisition, and we'll have her on the programme."

"What mystery?" Mr. Banks asked.

" Oh, well, not mystery, maybe, but we all suppose she's not happy. How could she be with so
few of the real pleasures of life, and still she
stays with it, and actually goes places with her
husband, and seems to be keeping it up, and you
know, Ted, she has either three or four children!"

" Is it as bad as that?" he asked, solemnly.

" Oh, Ted! you know well enough what I mean
—don't be such an owl! Just think of how tied
down and horrible it must be for her out there
in that desolate Alberta, with no neighbors at
all for miles, and then only impossible people.
I should think it would drive her mad. I must
try to get her on the programme, too. She will
at least be interesting, on account of her person-
ality. Most of our speakers are horribly prosy,
at least to me, but of course I never listen; I just
look to see what they've on and then go straight
back to my own thinking. I just thought I'd
ask your advice, Teddy dear, before I asked the
Committee, and so now I'll go to see Mrs. Trenton, the President. So glad you approve, dear!
And really there will be a touch of romance in it,
Ted, for Bruce Edwards knew her when she lived
in Ottawa—it was he who told me so much about
her. He simply raved about her to me—it seems
he was quite mad about her once, and probably
it was a lover's quarrel or something that drove
her away to the West to forget,—and now think

of her meeting Bruce again. Isn't that a thriller?"

"If I thought Bruce Edwards had brains enough to care for any woman I'd say it was not right to bring her here," said Mr. Banks; " but he hasn't."

" Oh, of course," Mrs. Banks agreed, " he is quite over it now, no doubt. Things like that never last, but he'll be awfully nice to her, and give her a good time and take her around—you know what Bruce is like—he's so romantic and cynical, and such a perfect darling in his manners—always ready to open a door or pick up a handkerchief!"

" I am sure he would—if he needed the handkerchief," Theodore put in, quietly.

" Oh, Ted! you're a funny bunny! You've never liked Bruce—and I know why—and it's perfectly horrid of you, just because he has always been particularly nice to me—he really can't help being dreamy and devoted to any woman he is with, if she is not a positive fright."

.   .   .   .

Mrs. Trenton, the President of the Arts and Crafts, received Mrs. Banks' suggestion cautiously. Mrs. Trenton always asked, Is it right? Is it wise? Is it expedient? It was Mrs. Trenton's extreme cautiousness that had brought her the proud distinction of being the first President of the Arts and Crafts, where it was considered necessary to temper . the impetuosity of the younger members; and, besides, Mrs. Trenton never carried her doubts and fears too far. She raised all possible objections, mentioned all possible contingencies, but in the end allowed the younger members to carry the day, which they did, with a clear and shriven conscience, feeling that they had been very discreet and careful and deliberate.

Mrs. Banks introduced her subject by telling Mrs. Trenton that she had come to ask her advice, whereupon Mrs. Trenton laid aside the work she was doing and signified her gracious willingness to be asked for counsel. When Mrs. Banks had carefully laid the matter before Mrs. Trenton, dwelling on the utter loneliness of the prairie woman's life, Mrs. Trenton called the Vice-President, Miss Hastings, who was an oil painter by profession, and a lady of large experience in matters of the heart. Mrs. Trenton asked Mrs Banks to outline her plan again.

When she had finished, Mrs. Trenton asked: " Is it wise—is it kind? She has chosen her life. Why bring her back? It will only fill her heart with vain repinings. This man, illiterate though he may be, is her lawful husband—she owes him a duty. Are we just to him?"

"Maybe she is perfectly happy," Miss Hastings said. "There is no accounting for love and its vagaries. Perhaps to her he is clothed in the rosy glow of romance, and all the inconveniences of her life are forgotten   I have read of it," she added in explanation, when she noticed Mrs. Trenton's look of incredulity.

Mrs. Trenton sighed, a long sigh that undu- lated the black lace on her capacious bosom.

"It has been written—it will continue to be written, but to-day marriage needs to be aided by modern—" she hesitated, and looked at Mrs. Banks for the word.

"Methods," Mrs. Banks supplied, promptly, " housemaids, cooks, autos, theatres, jewelry and chocolates."

"You put it so aptly, my dear," Mrs. Trenton smiled, as she patted her pearl bracelet, Mr. Trenton's last offering on the hymeneal altar. "It requires—" she paused again—Mrs. Tren- ton's pauses were a very important asset in her conversation—"it requires—"

"Collateral," said Mrs. Banks.

Miss Hastings shook her head.

"I believe in marriage—all the same," she said heroically.

"Now, how shall we do it?" Mrs. Banks was anxious to get the preliminaries over. "You have decided to invite her, of course."

Mrs. Trenton nodded.

"I feel we have no choice in the matter," she said slowly. "She is certainly a woman of artistic temperament—she must be, or she would

succumb to the dreary prairie level. I have followed her career with interest and predict great
things for her—have I not, Miss Hastings? We
should not blame her if in a moment of girlish
romance she turned her back on the life which
now is. We, as officers of the Arts and Crafts,
must extend our fellowship to all who are
worthy. This joining of our ranks may show
her what she lost by her girlish folly, but it is
better for her to know life, and even feel regrets,
than never to know."

" Better have a scarlet thread run through the
dull gray pattern of life, even if it makes the
gray all the duller," said Miss Hastings, who
worked in oils.

And so it came about that an invitation was
sent to Mrs. James Dawson, Auburn, Alberta,
and in due time an acceptance was received.

From the time she alighted from the Pacific
Express, a slight young woman in a very smart
linen suit, she was a constant surprise to the
Arts and Crafts. The principal cause of their
surprise was that she seemed perfectly happy.
There was not a shadow of regret in her clear
grey eyes, nor any trace of drooping melancholy
in her quick, business-like walk.

Naturally the Arts and Crafts had made quite
a feature of the Alberta author and poet who
would attend the Convention. Several of the
enthusiastic members, anxious to advertise effec-

tively, had interviewed the newspaper reporters on the subject, with the result that long articles were published in the Woman's Section of the city dailies, dealing principally with the loneliness of the life on an Alberta ranch Kate Dawson was credited with an heroic spirit that would have made her blush had she seen the flattering allusions. Robinson Crusoe on his lonely isle, before the advent of Friday, was not more isolated than she on her lonely Alberta ranch, according to the advance notices. Luckily she had not seen any of these, nor ever dreamed she was the centre of so much attention, and so it was a very self-possessed and unconscious young woman in a simple white gown who came before the Arts and Crafts.

It was the first open night of the Convention, and the auditorium was crowded. The air was heavy with the perfume of many flowers, and pulsed with dreamy music. Mrs. Trenton, in billows of black lace and glinting jet, presided with her usual graciousness. She introduced Mrs. Dawson briefly.

Whatever the attitude of the audience was at first, they soon followed her with eager interest as she told them, in her easy way, simple stories of the people she knew so well and so lovingly understood. There was no art in the telling, only a sweet naturalness and an apparent honesty—the honesty of purpose that comes to people in lonely places. Her stories were all of the class that magazine editors call "homely, heart-interest stuff," not deep or clever or problematical—the commonplace doings of common people—but it found an entrance into the hearts of men and women.

They found themselves looking with her at broad sunlit spaces, where struggling hearts work out noble destinies, without any thought of heroism. They saw the moonlight and its drifting shadows on the wheat, and smelled again the ripening grain at dawn. They heard the whirr of prairie chickens' wings among the golden stubble on the hillside, and the glamor of some old forgotten afternoon stole over them. Men and women country-born who had forgotten the voices of their youth, heard them calling across the years, and heard them, too, with opened hearts and sudden tears. There was one pathetic story she told them, of the lonely prairie woman—the woman who wished she was back, the woman to whom the broad outlook and far horizon were terrible and full of fear. She told them how, at night, this lonely woman drew down the blinds and pinned them close to keep out the great white outside that stared at her through every chink with wide, pitiless eyes— the mocking voices that she heard behind her everywhere, day and night, whispering, mocking, plotting; and the awful shadows, black ·and terrible, that crouched behind her, just out of sight—never coming out in the open.

It was a weird and gloomy picture, that, but she did not leave it so. She told of the new neighbor who came to live near the lonely woman —the human companionship which drove the mocking voices away forever—the coming of the spring, when the world awoke from its white sleep and the thousand joyous living things that came into being at the touch of the good old sun!

At the reception after the programme, many crowded around her, expressing their sincere appreciation of her work. Bruce Edwards fully enjoyed the distinction which his former acquaintance with her gave him, and it was with quite an air of proprietorship that he introduced to her his friends.

Mrs. Trenton, Mrs. Banks and other members of the Arts and Crafts, at a distance discussed her with pride. She had made their open night a wonderful success—the papers would be full of it to-morrow.

"You can see how fitted she is for a life of culture," said Miss Hastings, the oil painter; "her shapely white hands were made for silver spoons, and not for handling butter ladles. What a perfect joy it must be for her to associate with people who are her equals!"

"I wonder," said Mrs. Banks, "what her rancher would say if he saw his handsome wife now. So much admiration from an old lover is not good for the peace of mind of even a serious-minded author—and such a fascinating man as Bruce! Look how well they look together! I wonder if she is mentally comparing her big, sunburned cattleman with Bruce, and thinking of what a different life she would have led if she had married him!"

"Do you suppose," said Mrs. Trenton, "that that was her own story that she told us? I think she must have felt it herself to be able to tell it so."

Just at that moment Bruce Edwards was asking her the same question.

"Oh, no," she answered, quickly, while an interested group drew near; "people never write their own sorrows—the broken heart does not sing—that's the sadness of it. If one can talk of their sorrows they soon cease to be. It's because I have not had any sorrows of my own that I have seen and been able to tell of the tragedies of life."

"Isn't she the jolly best bluffer you ever heard?" one of the men remarked to another. "Just think of that beautiful creature, born for admiration, living ten miles from anywhere, on an Albertan ranch of all places, and saying she is happy. She could be a top-notcher in any society in Canada—why, great Scott! any of us would have married that girl, and been glad to

169

do it!" And under the glow of this generous declaration Mr. Stanley Carruthers lit his cigarette and watched her with unconcealed admiration.

As the Arts and Crafts had predicted, the newspapers gave considerable space to their open meeting, and the Alberta author came in for a large share of the reporters' finest spasms. It was the chance of a lifetime—here was local color—human interest—romance—thrills! Good old phrases, clover-scented and rosy-hued, that had lain in cold storage for years, were brought out and used with conscious pride.

There was one paper which boldly hinted at what it called her *"mesalliance,"* and drew a lurid picture of her domestic unhappiness, "so bravely borne." All the gossip of the Convention was in it intensified and exaggerated—conjectures set down as known truths—the idle chatter of idle women crystallized in print!

And of this paper a copy was sent by some unknown person to James Dawson, Auburn, Alberta.

.   .   .   .

The rain was falling at Auburn, Alberta, with the dreary insistence of unwelcome harvest rain. Just a quiet drizzle—plenty more where this came from—no haste, no waste. It soaked the fields, keeping green the grain which should be ripening in a clear sun.

YOU NEVER CAN TELL

Kate Dawson had been gone a week, and it would still be a week before she came back Just a week—seven days. Jim Dawson went over them in his mind as he drove the ten miles over the rain-soaked roads to Auburn to get his daily letter.

Every day she had written to him long letters, full of vital interest to him. He read them over and over again.

"Nobody really knows how well Kate can write, who has not seen her letters to me," he thought proudly. Absence had not made him fonder of his wife, for every day he lived was lived in devotion to her. The marvel of it all never left him, that such a woman as Kate Marks, who had spent her life in the city, surrounded by cultured friends, should be contented to live the lonely life of a rancher's wife.

He got his first disappointment when there was no letter for him. He told himself it was some unavoidable delay in the mails—Kate had written all right—there would be two letters for him to-morrow. Then he noticed the paper addressed to him in a strange hand.

He opened it eagerly. A wavy ink-line caught his eye. "Western author delights large audience." Jim Dawson's face glowed with pride "My girl!" he murmured, happily. "I knew it." He wanted to be alone when he read it, and, folding it hastily, put it in his pocket and did not look at it again until he was on the way home. The rain still fell drearily and spattered the page as he read.

His heart beat fast with pride as he read the flattering words—his girl had made good, you bet!

Suddenly he started, almost crushing the paper in his hands, and every bit of color went from his face. "What's this? 'Unhappily married'—'borne with heroic cheerfulness.'" He read it through to the end.

He stopped his horses and looked around—he did not know, himself, what thought was in his mind. Jim Dawson had always been able to settle his disputes without difficulty or delay. There was something to be done now. The muscles swelled in his arms. Surely something could be done! . . .

Then the wanton cruelty, the utter brutality of the printed page came home to him—there was no way, no answer.

Strange to say, he felt no resentment for himself; even the paragraph about the old lover, with its hidden and sinister meaning, angered him only in its relation to her. Why shouldn't the man admire her if he was an old lover?—Kate must have had dozens of men in love with her—why shouldn't any man admire her?

So he talked and reasoned with himself, trying to keep the cruel hurt of the words out of his heart.

Everyone in his household was asleep when he reached home. He stabled his team with the help of his lantern, and then, going into the comfortable kitchen, he found the lunch the housekeeper had left for him. He thought of the many merry meals he and Kate had had on this same kitchen table, but now it seemed a poor, cold thing to sit down and eat alone and in silence.

With his customary thoughtfulness he cleared away the lunch before going to his room. Then, lamp in hand, he went, as he and Kate had always done, to the children's room, and looked long and lovingly at his boy and girl asleep in their cots—the boy so like himself, with his broad forehead and brown curls. He bent over him and kissed him tenderly—Kate's boy.

Then he turned to the little girl, so like her mother, with her tangle of red curls on the pillow. Picking her up in his arms, he carried her to his room and put her in his own bed.

"Mother isn't putting up a bluff on us, is she, dearie?" he whispered as he kissed the soft little cheek beside his own. "Mother loves us, surely—it is pretty rough on us if she doesn't—and it's rougher still on mother!"

The child stirred in her sleep, and her arms tightened around his neck.

YOU NEVER CAN TELL

"I love my mother—and my dear daddy," she murmured drowsily.

All night long Jim Dawson lay wide-eyed, staring into the darkness with his little sleeping girl in his arms, not doubting his wife for a moment, but wondering—all night long—wondering!

The next evening Jim did not go for his mail, but one of the neighbors driving by volunteered to get it for him.

It was nearly midnight when the sound of wheels roused him from his reverie. He opened the door, and in the square of light the horses stopped.

"Hello, Jim—is that you?" called the neighbor; "I've got something for you."

Jim came out bareheaded. He tried to thank the neighbor for his kindness, but his throat was dry with suppressed excitement—Kate had written!

The buggy was still in the shadow, and he could not see its occupant.

"I have a letter for you, Jim," said his friend, with a suspicious twinkle in his voice, "a big one, registered and special delivery—a right nice letter, I should say."

Then her voice rang out in the darkness.

"Come, Jim, and help me out."

Commonplace words, too, but to Jim Dawson

they were sweeter than the chiming of silver
bells. . . . .

An hour later they still sat over their late
supper on the kitchen table. She had told him
many things.

"I just got lonely, Jim—plain, straight homesick for you and the children. I couldn't stay
out the week. The people were kind to me, and
said nice things about my work. I was glad to
hear and see things, of course. Bruce Edwards
was there, you know—I've told you about Bruce.
He took me around quite a bit, and was nice
enough, only I couldn't lose him—you know that
kind, Jim, always saying tiresome, plastery sort
of things. He thinks that women like to be
fussed over all the time. The women I met dress
beautifully and all talk the same—and at once.
Everything is 'perfectly sweet' and 'darling'
to them. They are clever women all right, and
were kind to me, and all that, but oh, Jim, they
are not for mine—and the men I met while I
was away all looked small and poor and trifling
to me because I have been looking for the last
ten years at one who is big and brown and useful.
I compared them all with you, and they mea-
sured up badly. Jim, do you know what it would
feel like to live on popcorn and chocolates for
two weeks and try to make a meal of them—what
do you think you would be hungry for?"

Jim Dawson. watched his wife, his eyes aglow with love and pride. Not until she repeated her question did he answer her.

" I think, perhaps, a slice of brown bread would be what was wanted," he answered smiling. The glamor of her presence was upon him.

Then she came over to him and drew his face close to hers.

" Please pass the brown bread!" she said.

A SHORT TALE OF A RABBIT

A Short Tale of a Rabbit

(Reprinted by permission of *Canada West Monthly.*)

JOHNNY was the only John rabbit in the family that lived in the poplar bluff in the pasture. He had a bold and adventurous spirit, but was sadly hampered by his mother's watchfulness. She was as full of warnings as the sign-board at the railway crossing. It was " Look out for the cars!" all the time with mother. She warned him of dogs and foxes, hawks and snakes, boys and men. It was in vain that Johnny showed her his paces —how he could leap and jump and run. She admitted that he was quite a smart little rabbit for his age, but—oh, well! you know what mothers are like.

Johnny was really tired of it, and then, too, Johnny had found out that what mother had said about dogs was very much exaggerated. Johnny had met two dogs, so he thought he knew something about them. One was a sleek, fat, black puppy, with a vapid smile, called Juno; and the other was an amber-eyed spaniel with woolly, fat legs. They had run after Johnny one day when he was out playing on the road, and he had led

179

them across a ploughed field. Johnny was accustomed to add, as he told the story to the young rabbits that lived down in the pasture, that he had to spurt around the field a few times after the race was over just to limber up his legs—he was so cramped from sitting around waiting for the dogs. So it came about that Johnny, in his poor, foolish little heart, thought dogs were just a joke.

Johnny's mother told him that all men were bad, and the men who carried guns were worst of all, for guns spit out fire and death. She said there were men who wore coats the color of dead grass, and drove in rigs that rattled and had dogs with them, and they killed ducks and geese that were away up in the air. She said those men drove miles and miles just to kill things, and they lived sometimes in a little house away out near the lakes where the ducks stayed, and they didn't mind getting up early in the morning or sitting up at night to get a shot at a duck, and when they got the ducks they just gave them away. If half what old Mrs. Rabbit said about them was true, they certainly were the Bad Men from Bitter Creek! Johnny listened, big-eyed, to all this, and there were times when he was almost afraid to go to bed. Still, when he found out that dogs were not so dangerous, he began to think his mother might have overstated the man question, too.

A SHORT TALE OF A RABBIT

One day Johnny got away from his mother, when she was busy training the other little rabbits in the old trick of dodging under the wire fence just when the dog is going to grab you. Johnny knew how it was done—it was as easy as rolling off a log for him, and so he ran away. He came up at the Agricultural Grounds. He had often been close to the fence before, but his mother had said decidedly he must never go in.

Just beside the gate he found a bread crust which was lovely, and there might be more, mightn't there? There wasn't a person in sight, or a dog. Johnny went a little farther in and found a pile of cabbage leaves—a pile of them, mind you—he really didn't know what to think of his mother—she certainly was the limit! Johnny grew bolder; a little farther on he found more bread crumbs and some stray lettuce leaves —he began to feel a little sorry for his mother— lettuce leaves, cabbage leaves and bread crumbs —and she had said, " Don't go in there, Johnny, whatever you do!"

The band was playing, and there were flags in the air, but Johnny didn't notice it. He didn't know, of course, that the final lacrosse match of the season was going to be played that afternoon. Johnny had just gone into one of the cattle sheds to see what was there, when a little boy, with flopped-out ears and a Cow Brand Soda cap on, stealthily closed the gate. Johnny didn't know he had on a Cow Brand Soda cap, and he didn't know that the gate was shut, but he did know that that kind of a yell meant business. He wasn't afraid. Pshaw! He'd give young Mr. Flop-Ears a run for his money. Come on, kid— r-r-r-r-r! Johnny ran straight to the gate with a rabbit's unerring instinct, and hurled himself against it in vain. The flop-eared boy screamed with laughter. Then there were more Boys. And Dogs. All screaming. The primitive savage in them was awake now. Here was a wild thing who defied them, with all his speed. Johnny was running now with his ears laid back, mad with terror, dogs barking, boys screaming, even men joining in the chase, for the lust for blood was on them. Again Johnny made the circuit of the field—the noise grew—a hundred voices, it seemed, not one that was friendly. It was one little throbbing rabbit against the field, with all the odds against him, running for his life, and losing! "Sic him, Togo! Sic him, Collie! Gee! Can't he run? But we've got him this time. He'll soon slow up." A dog snapped at him and his hind leg grew heavy. Some one struck at him with a lacrosse stick, and then—

He found himself running alone. Behind him a dog yelped with pain, and above the noise some-one shouted: " Here, you kids, let up on that! Shame on you! Let him alone! Call off your dogs, there! Poor little duffer, let him go. Get back there, Twin!"

Johnny ran dazed and dizzy, and once more made the circuit and dashed again for the gate. But this time the gate was open, and Johnny was free! Saved, and by whom?

Well, of course, old Mrs. Rabbit didn't believe a word of it when Johnny went home and told her who called off the dogs and opened the gate for him. She said,—well, she talked very plainly to Johnny, but he stuck to it, that he owed his life to one of the Bad Men who wear clothes the color of grass, and whose gun spits fire and death. For old Mrs. Rabbit made just the same mistake that many people make of thinking that a man that hunts must be cruel, forgetting that the true sportsman loves the wild things he makes war on, and though he kills them, he does it fairly and openly.

THE ELUSIVE VOTE

The Elusive Vote

AN UNVARNISHED TALE OF SEPTEMBER 21st, 1911

JOHN THOMAS GREEN did not look like a man
on whom great issues might turn. His was a
gentle soul encased in ill-fitting armour. Heavy
blue eyes, teary and sad, gave a wintry droop to
his countenance; his nose showed evidence of
much wiping, and the need of more. When he
spoke, which was infrequent, he stammered;
when he walked he toed in.

He was a great and glorious argument in favor
of woman suffrage; he was the last word, the
pièce de résistance; he was a living, walking,
yellow banner, which shouted "Votes for
Women," for in spite of his many limitations
there was one day when he towered high above
the mightiest woman in the land; one day that
the plain John Thomas was clothed with majesty
and power; one day when he emerged from
obscurity and placed an impress on the annals
of our country. Once every four years John
Thomas Green came forth (at the earnest solici-
tation of friends) and stood before kings.

187

THE ELUSIVE VOTE

The Reciprocity fight was on, and nowhere did it rage more hotly than in Morton, where Tom Brown, the well-beloved and much-hated Conservative member, fought for his seat with all the intensity of his Irish blood. Politics were an incident to Tom—the real thing was the fight! and so fearlessly did he go after his assailants—and they were many—that every day greater enthusiasm prevailed among his followers, who felt it a privilege to fight for a man who fought so well for himself.

The night before the election the Committee sat in the Committee Rooms and went carefully over the lists. They were hopeful but not hilarious—there had been disappointments, desertions, lapses!

Billy Weaver, loyal to the cause, but of pessimistic nature, testified that Sam Cowery had been "talkin' pretty shrewd about reciprocity," by which Billy did not mean "shrewd" at all, but rather crooked and adverse. However, there was no mistaking Billy's meaning of the word when one heard him say it with his inimitable "down-the-Ottaway" accent. It is only the feeble written word which requires explanation.

George Burns was reported to have said he did not care whether he voted or not; if it were a wet day he might, but if it were weather for stacking he'd stack, you bet! This was a gross insult to the President of the Conservative Association, whose farm he had rented and lived on for the last five years, during which time there had been two elections, at both of which he had voted " right." The President had not thought it necessary to interview him at all this time, feeling sure that he was within the pale. But now it seemed that some trifler had told him that he would get more for his barley and not have to pay so much for his tobacco if Reciprocity carried, and it was reported that he had been heard to say, with picturesque eloquence, that you could hardly expect a man to cut his throat both ways by voting against it!

These and other kindred reports filled the Committee with apprehension.

The most unmoved member of the company was the redoubtable Tom himself, who, stretched upon the slippery black leather lounge, hoarse as a frog from much addressing of obdurate electors, was endeavoring to sing " Just Before the Battle, Mother," hitting the tune only in the most inconspicuous places!

The Secretary, with the list in his hand, went over the names:

" Jim Stewart—Jim's solid; he doesn't want Reciprocity, because he sent to the States once for a washing-machine for his wife, and smuggled it through from St. Vincent, and when he got it here his wife wouldn't use it!

"Abe Collins—Abe's not right and never will be—he saw Sir Wilfrid once—

"John Thomas Green—say, how about Jack? Surely we can corral Jack. He's working for you, Milt, isn't he?" addressing one of the scrutineers.

"Leave him to me," said Milt, with an air of mystery; "there's no one has more influence with Jack than me. No, he isn't with me just now, he's over with my brother Angus; but when he comes in to vote I'll be there, and all I'll have to do is to lift my eyes like this" (he showed them the way it would be done) "and he'll vote —right"

"How do you know he will come, though?" asked the Secretary, who had learned by much experience that many and devious are the bypaths which lead away from the polls!

"Yer brother Angus will be sure to bring him in, won't he, Milt?" asked John Gray, the trusting one, who believed all men to be brothers.

There was a tense silence.

Milt took his pipe from his mouth. "My brother Angus," he began, dramatically, girding himself for the effort—for Milt was an orator of Twelfth of July fame—"Angus Kennedy, my brother, bred and reared, and reared and bred, in the principles of Conservatism, as my poor old father often says, has gone over—has deserted our banners, has steeped himself in the false teachings of the Grits. Angus, my brother," he concluded, impressively, "is—not right!"

"What's wrong with him?" asked Jim Grover, who was of an analytical turn of mind.

"Too late to discuss that now!" broke in the Secretary; "we cannot trace Angus's downfall, but we can send out and get in John Thomas. We need his vote—it's just as good as anybody's."

Jimmy Rice volunteered to go out and get him. Jimmy did not believe in leaving anything to chance. He had been running an auto all week and would just as soon work at night as any other time. Big Jack Moore, another enthusiastic Conservative, agreed to go with him.

When they made the ten-mile run to the home of the apostate Angus, they met him coming down the path with a lantern in his hand on the way to feed his horses.

They, being plain, blunt men, unaccustomed to the amenities of election time, and not knowing how to skilfully approach a subject of this kind, simply announced that they had come for John Thomas.

"He's not here," said Angus, looking around the circle of light that the lantern threw.

"Are you sure?" asked James Rice, after a painful pause.

"Yes," said Angus, with exaggerated ease, affecting not to notice the significance of the question. "Jack went to Nelson to-day, and he ain't back yet. He went about three o'clock," went on Angus, endeavoring to patch up a shaky story with a little interesting detail. " He took over a bunch of pigs for me that I am shippin' into Winnipeg, and he was goin' to bring back some lumber."

"I was in Nelson to-day, Angus," said John Moore, sternly; "just came from there, and I did not see John Thomas."

Angus, though fallen and misguided, was not entirely unregenerate; a lie sat awkwardly on his honest lips, and now that his feeble effort at deception had miscarried, he felt himself adrift on a boundless sea. He wildly felt around for a reply, and was greatly relieved by the arrival of his father on the scene, who, seeing the lights of the auto in the yard, had come out hurriedly to see what was the matter. Grandpa Kennedy, although nearing his ninetieth birthday, was still a man of affairs, and what was still more important on this occasion, a lifelong Conservative. Grandpa knew it was the night before the election; he also had seen what he had seen. Grandpa might be getting on, but he could see as far through a cellar door as the next one. Angus, glad of a chance to escape, went on to the stable, leaving the visiting gentlemen to be entertained by Grandpa.

Grandpa was a diplomat; he wanted to have no hard feelings with anyone.

"Good-night, boys," he cried, in his shrill voice; he recognized the occupants of the auto and his quick brain took in the situation. "Don't it beat all how the frost keeps off? This reminds me of the fall, 'leven years ago—we had no frost till the end of the month. I ripened three bushels of Golden Queen tomatoes!" All this was delivered in a very high voice for Angus's benefit—to show him, if he were listening, how perfectly innocent the conversation was.

Then as Angus's lantern disappeared behind the stable, the old man's voice was lowered, and he gave forth this cryptic utterance:

"John Thomas is in the cellar."

Then he gaily resumed his chatter, although Angus was safe in the stable; but Grandpa knew what he knew, and Angus's woman might be listening at the back door. "Much election talk in town, boys?" he asked, breezily.

They answered him at random. Then his voice fell again. "Angie's dead against Brown—won't let you have John Thomas—put him down cellar soon as he saw yer lights; Angie's woman is sittin on the door knittin'—she's wors'n him—don't let on I give it away—I don't want no words with her!—Yes, it's grand weather for threshin'; won't you come on away in? I guess yer horse will stand." The old man roared with laughter at his own joke.

John Moore and James Rice went back to headquarters for further advice. Angus's woman sitting on the cellar door knitting was a contingency that required to be met with guile.

Consternation sat on the face of the Committee when they told their story. They had not counted on this. The wildest plans were discussed. Tom Stubbins began a lengthy story of an elopement that happened down at the "Carp," where the bride made a rope of the sheets and came down from an upstairs window. Tom was not allowed to finish his narrative, though, for it was felt that the cases were not similar.

No one seemed to be particularly anxious to go back and interrupt Mrs. Angus's knitting.

Then there came into the assembly one of the latest additions to the Conservative ranks, William Batters, a converted and reformed Liberal. He had been an active member of the Liberal party for many years, but at the last election he had been entirely convinced of their unworthiness by the close-fisted and niggardly way in which they dispensed the election money.

He heard the situation discussed in all its aspects. Milton Kennedy, with inflamed oratory, bitterly bewailed his brother's defection—" not only wrong himself, but leadin' others, and them innocent lambs!"—but he did not offer to go out and see his brother. The lady who sat knitting on the cellar door seemed to be the difficulty with all of them.

The reformed Liberal had a plan.

"I will go for him," said he. "Angus will trust me—he doesn't know I have turned. I'll go for John Thomas, and Angus will give him to me without a word, thinkin' I'm a friend," he concluded, brazenly.

"Look at that now!" exclaimed the member elect. "Say, boys, you'd know he had been a Grit—no honest, open-faced Conservative would ever think of a trick like that!"

"There is nothing like experience to make a man able to see every side," said the reformed one, with becoming modesty.

An hour later Angus was roused from his bed by a loud knock on the door. Angus had gone to bed with his clothes on, knowing that these were troublesome times.

"What's the row?" he asked, when he had cautiously opened the door.

"Row!" exclaimed the friend who was no longer a friend, "You're the man that's makin' the row. The Conservatives have 'phoned in to the Attorney-General's Department to-night to see what's to be done with you for standin' between a man and his heaven-born birthright, keepin' and confinin' of a man in a cellar, owned by and closed by you!"

This had something the air of a summons, and Angus was duly impressed.

"I don't want to see you get into trouble. Angus," Mr. Batters went on; "and the only way to keep out of it is to give him to me, and then when they come out here with a search-warrant they won't find nothin'."

Angus thanked him warmly, and, going upstairs, roused the innocent John from his virtuous slumbers. He had some trouble persuading John, who was a profound sleeper, that he must arise and go hence; but many things were strange to him, and he rose and dressed without very much protest.

Angus was distinctly relieved when he got John Thomas off his hands—he felt he had had a merciful deliverance.

On the way to town, roused by the night air, John Thomas became communicative.

"Them lads in the automobile, they wanted me pretty bad, you bet," he chuckled, with the conscious pride of the much-sought-after; "but gosh, Angus fixed them. He just slammed down the cellar door on me, and says he, 'Not a word out of you, Jack; you've as good a right to vote the way you want to as anybody, and you'll get it, too, you bet.'"

THE ELUSIVE VOTE

The reformed Liberal knitted his brows. What was this simple child of nature driving at?

John Thomas rambled on: "Tom Brown can't fool people with brains, you bet you—Angus's woman explained it all' to me. She says to me, 'Don't let nobody run you, Jack—and vote for Hastings. You're all right, Jack—and remember Hastings is the man. Never mind why—don't bother your head—you don't have to—but vote for Hastings.' Says she, 'Don't let on to Milt, or any of his folks, or Grandpa, but vote the way you want to, and that's for Hastings!'"

When they arrived in town the reformed Liberal took John Thomas at once to the Conservative Hotel, and put him in a room, and told him to go to bed, which John cheerfully did. Then he went for the Secretary, who was also in bed. "I've got John Thomas," he announced, "but he says he's a Grit and is going to vote for Hastings. I can't put a dint in him—he thinks I'm a Grit, too. He's only got one idea, but it's a solid one, and that is 'Vote for Hastings.'"

The Secretary yawned sleepily. "I'll not go near him. It's me for sleep. You can go and see if any of the other fellows want a job. They're all down at a ball at the station. Get one of those wakeful spirits to reason with John."

The conspirator made his way stealthily to the station, from whence there issued the sound of

197

music and dancing. Not wishing to alarm the Grits, many of whom were joining in the festivities, and who would have been quick to suspect that something was on foot, if they saw him prowling around, he crept up to the window and waited until one of the faithful came near. Gently tapping on the glass, he got the attention of the editor, the very man he wanted, and, in pantomime, gave him to understand that his presence was requested. The editor, pleading a terrific headache, said good-night, or rather good-morning, to his hostess, and withdrew. From his fellow-worker who waited in the shadow of the trees outside, he learned that John Thomas had been secured in the body but not in spirit.

The newspaper man readily agreed to labor with the erring brother and hoped to be able to deliver his soul alive.

Once again was John Thomas roused from his slumbers, and not by a familiar voice this time, but by an unknown vision in evening dress.

The editor was a convincing man in his way, whether upon the subject of reciprocity or apostolic succession, but John was plainly bored from the beginning, and though he offered no resistance, his repeated " I know that!" " That's what I said!" were more disconcerting than the most vigorous opposition. At daylight the editor left John, and he really had the headache that he had feigned a few hours before.

Then John Thomas tried to get a few winks of unmolested repose, but it was election day, and the house was early astir. Loud voices sounded through the hall. Innumerable people, it seemed, mistook his room for their own. Jack rose at last, thoroughly indignant and disposed to quarrel. He had a blame good notion to vote for Brown after all, after the way he had been treated.

When he had hastily dressed himself, discussing his grievances in a loud voice, he endeavored to leave the room, but found the door securely locked. Then his anger knew no bounds. He lustily kicked on the lower panel of the door and fairly shrieked his indignation and rage.

The chambermaid, passing, remonstrated with him by beating on the other side of the door. She was a pert young woman with a squeaky voice, and she thought she knew what was wrong with the occupant of 17. She had heard kicks on doors before.

"Quiet down, you, mister, or you'll get yourself put in the cooler—that's the best place for noisy drunks."

This, of course, annoyed the innocent man beyond measure, but she was gone far down the hall before he could think of the retort suitable.

When she finished her upstairs work and came downstairs to peel the potatoes, she mentioned casually to the bartender that whoever he had in number 17 was "smashin' things up pretty lively!"

The bartender went up and liberated the indignant voter, who by this time had his mind made up to vote against both Brown and Hastings, and furthermore to renounce politics in all its aspects for evermore.

However, a good breakfast and the sincere apologies of the hotel people did much to restore his good humor. But a certain haziness grew in his mind as to who was who, and at times the disquieting thought skidded through his murky brain that he might be in the enemy's camp for all he knew. Angus and Mrs. Angus had said, "Do what you think is right and vote for Hastings," and that was plain and simple and easily understood. But now things seemed to be all mixed up.

The committee were ill at ease about him. The way he wagged his head and declared he knew what was what, you bet, was very disquieting, and the horrible fear haunted them that they were perchance cherishing a serpent in their bosom.

The Secretary had a proposal: "Take him out to Milt Kennedy's. Milt said he could work him. Take him out there! Milt said all he had to do was to raise his eyes and John Thomas would vote right."

The erstwhile Liberal again went on the road

with John Thomas, to deliver him over to the authority of Milt Kennedy. If Milt could get results by simply elevating his eyebrows, Milt was the man who was needed.

Arriving at Milt's, he left the voter sitting in the buggy, while he went in search of the one who could control John's erring judgment.

While sitting there alone, another wandering thought zig-zagged through John's brain. They were making a fool of him, some way! Well, he'd let them see, b'gosh!

He jumped out of the buggy, and hastily climbed into the hay-mow. It was a safe and quiet spot, and was possessed of several convenient eye-holes through which he could watch with interest the search which immediately began.

He saw the two men coming up to the barn, and as they passed almost below him, he heard Milt say, "Oh, sure, John Thomas will vote right—I can run him all right!—he'll do as I say. Hello, John! Where is he?"

They went into the house—they searched the barn—they called, coaxed, entreated. They ran down to the road to see if he had started back to town; he was as much gone as if he had never been!

"Are you dead sure you brought him?" Milt asked at last in desperation, as he turned over a pile of sacks in the granary.

THE ELUSIVE VOTE

"Gosh! ain't they lookin' some!" chuckled the elusive voter, as he watched with delight their unsuccessful endeavors to locate him. "But there's lots of places yet that they hain't thought of; they hain't half looked for me yet. I may be in the well for all they know." Then he began to sing to himself, "I know something I won't tell!"

It was not every day that John Thomas Green found himself the centre of attraction, and he enjoyed the sensation.

Having lost so much sleep the night before, a great drowsiness fell on John Thomas, and curling himself up in the hay, he sank into a sweet, sound sleep.

While he lay there, safe from alarms, the neighborhood was shaken with a profound sensation. John Thomas was lost. Lost, and his vote lost with him!

Milton Kennedy, who had to act as scrutineer at the poll in town, was forced to leave home with the mystery unsolved. Before going, he 'phoned to Billy Adams, one of the faithful, and in guarded speech, knowing that he was surrounded by a cloud of witnesses, broke the news! Billy Adams immediately left his stacking, and set off to find his lost compatriot.

Mrs. Alex Porter lived on the next farm to Billy Adams, and being a lady of some leisure, she usually managed to get in on most of the 'phone conversations. Billy Adams' calls were very seldom overlooked by her, for she was on the other side of politics, and it was always well to know what was going on. Although she did not know all that was said by the two men, she heard enough to assure her that crooked work was going on. Mrs. Alex Porter declared she was not surprised. She threw her apron over her head and went to the field and told Alex. Alex was not surprised. In fact, it seems Alex had expected it!

They 'phoned in cipher to Angus, Mrs Angus being a sister of Mrs. Alex Porter. Mrs. Angus told them to speak out plain, and say what they wanted to, even if all the Conservatives on the line were listening. Then Mrs. Porter said that John Thomas was lost over at Milt Kennedy's. They had probably drugged him or something.

Then Angus's wife said he was safe enough. Billy Batters had come and got him the night before. At the mention of Billy Batters there was a sound of suppressed mirth all along the line. Mrs. Angus's sister fairly shrieked. " Billy Batters! Don't you know he has turned Conservative!—he's working tooth and nail for Brown." Mrs. Angus called Angus excitedly. Everybody talked at once; somebody laughed; one or two swore. Mrs. Porter told Milt Kennedy's wife she'd caught her eavesdropping this time sure. She'd know her cackle any place, and Milt's wife told Mrs. Porter to shut up—she needn't talk about eavesdroppers,—good land! and Mrs. Porter told Mrs. Milt she should try something for that voice of hers, and recommended machine oil, and Central rang in and told them they'd all have their 'phones taken out if they didn't stop quarreling; and John Thomas, in the hay-mow, slept on, as peacefully as an innocent babe!

In the committee rooms, Jack's disappearance was excitedly discussed. The Conservatives were not sure that Bill Batters was not giving them the double cross—once a Grit, always a Grit! Angus was threatening to have him arrested for abduction—he had beguiled John Thomas from the home of his friends, and then carelessly lost him.

William Batters realized that he had lost favor in both places, and anxiously longed for a sight of John Thomas's red face, vote or no vote.

At four o'clock John Thomas awoke much refreshed, but very hungry. He went into the house in search of something to eat. Milton and his wife had gone into town many hours before, but he found what he wanted, and was going back to the hay-mow to finish his sleep, just as Billy Adams was going home after having cast his vote.

Billy Adams seized him eagerly, and rapidly drove back to town. Jack's vote would yet be saved to the party!

It was with pardonable pride that Billy Adams reined in his foaming team, and rushed John

Thomas into the polling booth, where he was greeted with loud cheers. Nobody dare ask him where he had been—time was too precious. Milton Kennedy, scrutineer, lifted his eyebrows as per agreement. Jack replied with a petulant shrug of his good shoulder and passed in to the inner chamber.

The Conservatives were sure they had him. The Liberals were sure, too. Mrs. Angus was sure Jack would vote right after the way she had reasoned with him and showed him!

When the ballots were counted, there were several spoiled ones, of course. But there was one that was rather unique. After the name of Thomas Brown, there was written in lead pencil, "*None of yer business!*" which might have indicated a preference for the other name of John Hastings, only for the fact that opposite his name was the curt remark, "*None of yer business, either!*"

Some thought the ballot was John Thomas Green's.

THE WAY OF THE WEST

The Way of the West

(Reprinted by permission of *The Globe*, Toronto.)

THOMAS SHOULDICE was displeased, sorely, bitterly displeased: in fact, he was downright mad, and being an Irish Orangeman, this means that he was ready to fight. You can imagine just how bitterly Mr. Shouldice was incensed when you hear that the Fourth of July had been celebrated with flourish of flags and blare of trumpets right under his very nose—in Canada —in British dominions!

The First of July, the day that should have been given up to "doin's," including the race for the greased pig, the three-legged race, and a ploughing match, had passed into obscurity, without so much as a pie-social; and it had rained that day, too, in torrents, just as if Nature herself did not care enough about the First to try to keep it dry.

The Fourth came in a glorious day, all sunshine and blue sky, with birds singing in every poplar bluff, and it was given such a celebration as Thomas had never seen since the "Twelfth" had been held in Souris. The

THE WAY OF THE WEST

American settlers who had been pouring into the Souris valley had—without so much as asking leave from the Government at Ottawa, the school trustees, or the oldest settler, who was Thomas himself—gone ahead and celebrated. Every American family had brought their own flagpole, in "joints," with them, and on the Fourth immense banners of stars and stripes spread their folds in triumph on the breeze.

The celebration was held in a large grove just across the road from Thomas Shouldice's little house; and to his inflamed patriotism, every fire-cracker that split the air, every cheer that rent the heavens, every blare of their smashing band music, seemed a direct challenge to King Edward himself, God bless him!

Mr. Shouldice worked all day at his hay-meadow, just to show them! He worked hard, too, never deigning a glance at their "carryin's on," just to let them know that he did not care two cents for their Fourth of July.

His first thought was to feign indifference, but when he saw the Wilsons, the Wrays, the Henrys, Canadian-bred and born, driving over to the enemy's camp, with their Sunday clothes on and big boxes of provisions on the "doggery" of their buckboards, his indifference fled and was replaced by profanity. It comforted him a little when he reflected that not an Orangeman had gone. They were loyal sons and true, every one of them. These other ignorant Canadians might forget what they owed to the old flag, but the Orangemen—never.

Thomas's rage against the Yankees was intensified when he saw Father O'Flynn walking across the plover slough. Then he was sure that the Americans and Catholics were in league against the British.

A mighty thought was conceived that day in the brain of Thomas Shouldice, late Worshipful Master of the Carleton Place Loyal Orange Lodge No. 23. They would celebrate the Twelfth, so they would; he'd like to see who would stop them. Someone would stand up for the flag that had braved a thousand years of battle and the breeze. He blew his nose noisily on his red handkerchief when he thought of this.

They would celebrate the Twelfth! They would "walk." He would gather up "the boys" and get someone to make a speech. They would get a fifer from Brandon. It was the fife that could stir the heart in you! And the fifer would play "The Protestant Boys" and "Rise, Sons of William, Rise!" Anyone that tried to stop him would get a shirt full of sore bones!

Thomas went home full of the plan to get back at the invaders! Rummaging through his trunk, he found, carefully wrapped with chewing tobacco and ground cedar, to keep the moths away, the regalia that he had worn, proudly and defiantly, once in Montreal, when the crowd that obstructed the triumphal march of the Orange Young Britons had to be dispersed by the "melitia." It was a glorious day, and one to be remembered with pride, for there had been shots fired and heads smashed.

His man, a guileless young Englishman, came in from mowing, gaily whistling the refrain the Yankee band had been playing at intervals all afternoon. It was "Dixie Land," and at first Thomas did not notice it. Rousing at last to the sinister significance of the tune, he ordered its cessation, in rosy-hued terms, and commended all such Yankee tunes and those that whistled them to that region where popular rumor has it that pots boil with or without watching.

Thomas Shouldice had lived by himself for a number of years. It was supposed that he had a wife living somewhere in "the States," which term to many Canadians indicates a shadowy region where bad boys, unfaithful wives and absconding embezzlers find refuge and dwell in dim security.

Thomas's devotion to the Orange Order was nothing short of a passion. He believed that but for its institution and perpetuation Protestant blood would flow like water. He always spoke of the "Stuarts" in an undertone, as if he were afraid they might even yet come back and make "rough house" for King Edward.

There were only two Catholic families in the neighborhood, and peaceable, friendly people they were, too; but Thomas believed they should be intimidated to prevent trouble. "The old spite is in them," he told himself, "and nothing will show them where they stand like a ' walk.' "

The next day Thomas left his haying and rounded up the faithful. There were seven members of the order in the community, all of whom were willing to stand for their country's honor. There was James Shewfelt, who was a drummer, and could play the tunes without the fife at all. There was John Barker, who did a musical turn in the form of a twenty-three verse ballad beginning:

"When Popery did flourish in
  Dear Ireland o'er the sea,
There came a man from Amsterdam
  To set ould Ireland free!
To set ould Ireland free, boys,
  To set ould Ireland free,—
There came a man from Amsterdam
  To set ould Ireland free!"

There was William Breeze, who was a little hard of hearing, but loyal to the core. He had seven boys in his family, so there was still hope for the nation. There was Patrick Mooney, who should have been wearing the other color if there is anything in a name. But there isn't. There was John Burns, who had been an engineer, but, having lost a foot, had taken to farming. He was the farthest advanced in the order next to Thomas Shouldice, having served a term as District Grand Master, and was well up in the Grand Black Chapter. These would form the nucleus of the procession. The seven little Breezes would be admitted to the ranks if their mother could find suitable decoration for them. Of course, the weather was warm and the subject of clothing was not so serious as it might have been.

Thomas drove nineteen miles to the nearest town to get a speaker and a fifer. The fifer was found, and, quite fortunately, was open for engagement. The speaker was not so easily secured. Thomas went to the Methodist missionary. The missionary was quite a young man and had the reputation of being an orator. He listened gravely while his visitor unfolded his plan.

"I'll tell you what to do, Mr. Shouldice," he said, smiling, when the other had finished the recital of his country's wrongs. "Get Father O'Flynn; he'll make you a speech that will do you all good."

Thomas was too astonished for words. "But he's a Papist!" he sputtered at last.

"Oh, pshaw! Oh, pshaw! Mr. Shouldice," the young man exclaimed; "there's no division of creed west of Winnipeg. The little priest does all my sick visiting north of the river, and I do his on the south. He's a good preacher, and the finest man at a deathbed I ever saw."

"This is not a deathbed, though, as it happens," Thomas replied, with dignity.

The young minister threw back his head and laughed uproariously. "Can't tell that until it is over—I've been at a few Orange walks down East, you know—took part in one myself once."

"Did you walk?" Thomas asked, brightening.

"No, I ran," the minister said, smiling.

"I thought you said you took part," Thomas snorted, with displeasure.

"So I did, but mine was a minor part. I stood behind the fence and helped the Brennan boys and Patrick Costigan to peg at them!"

"Are ye a Protestant at all?" Thomas roared at him, now thoroughly angry.

"Yes, I am," the minister said, slowly, "and I am something better still; I am a Christian and a Canadian. Are you?"

Thomas beat a hasty retreat.

The Presbyterian minister was away from home, and the English Church minister—who was also a young man lately arrived—said he would go gladly.

THE WAY OF THE WEST

The Twelfth of July was a beautiful day, clear, sparkling and cloudless. Little wayward breezes frolicked up and down the banks of Moose Creek and rasped the surface of its placid pools, swollen still from the heavy rains of the " First." In the glittering sunshine the prairie lay a riot of color; the first wild roses now had faded to a pastel pink, but on every bush there were plenty of new ones, deeply crimson and odorous. Across the creek from Thomas Shouldice's little house, Indian pipes and columbine reddened the edge of the poplar grove, from the lowest branches of which morning-glories, white and pink and purple, hung in graceful profusion.

Before noon a wagon filled with people came thundering down the trail. As they came nearer Thomas was astonished to see that it was an American family from the Chippen Hill district.

" Picnic in these parts, ain't there?" the driver asked.

Thomas was in a genial mood, occasioned by the day and the weather.

" Orange walk and picnic!" he replied, waving his hand toward the bluff, where a few of the faithful were constructing a triumphal arch.

" Something like a cake-walk, is it?" the man asked, looking puzzled.

Mr. Shouldice stared at him incredulously.

216

"Did ye never hear of Orangemen down yer way?" he said.

"Never did, pard," the man answered. "We've peanut men, and apple women, and banana men, but we've never heard much about orange men. But we're right glad to come over and help the show along. Do you want any money for the races?"

"We didn't count on havin' races; we're havin' speeches and some singin'."

The Yankee laughed good-humoredly.

"Well, friend, I pass there; but mother here is a W. C. T. U.-er from away back. She'll knock the spots off the liquor business in fifteen minutes, if you'd like anything in that line."

His wife interposed in her easy, drawling tones: "Now, Abe, you best shet up and drive along. The kids are all hungry and want their dinners."

"We'll see you later, partner," said the man as they drove away.

Thomas Shouldice was mystified. "These Americans are a queer bunch," he thought; "they're ignorant as all get out, but, gosh! they're friendly."

Over the hill to the south came other wagons filled with jolly picnickers, who soon had their pots boiling over quickly-constructed tripods.

Thomas, who went over to welcome them, found that nearly all of them were the very

THE WAY OF THE WEST

Americans whose unholy zeal for their own national holiday had so embittered his heart eight days before.

They were full of enquiries as to the meaning of an Orange walk. Thomas tried to explain, but, having only inflamed Twelfth of July oratory for the source of his information, he found himself rather at a loss. But the Americans gathered that it was something he used to do "down East," and they were sympathetic at once.

"That's right, you bet," one gray-haired man with a young face exclaimed, getting rid of a bulky chew of tobacco that had slightly impeded his utterance. "There's nothin' like keepin' up old institootions."

By two o'clock fully one hundred people had gathered.

Thomas was radiant. "Every wan is here now except that old Papist, O'Flynn," he whispered to the drummer. "I hope he'll come, too, so I do. It'll be a bitter pill for him to swallow."

The drummer did not share the wish. He was thinking, uneasily, of the time two years ago—the winter of the deep snow—when he and his family had been quarantined with smallpox, and of how Father O'Flynn had come miles out of his way every week on his snowshoes to hand in a roll of newspapers he had gathered up, no one knows where, and a bag of candies for the

218

little ones. He was thinking of how welcome the priest's little round face had been to them all those long, tedious six weeks, and how cheery his voice sounded as he shouted, "Are ye needin' anything, Jimmy, avick? All right, I'll be back on Thursda', God willin'. Don't be frettin', now, man alive! Everybody has to have the smallpox. Sure, yer shaming the Catholics this year, Jimmy, keeping Lent so well." The drummer was decidedly uneasy.

There is an old saying about speaking of angels in which some people still believe. Just at this moment Father O'Flynn came slowly over the hill.

Father O'Flynn was a typical little Irish priest, good-natured, witty, emotional. Nearly every family north of the river had some cause for loving the little man. He was a tireless walker, making the round of his parish every week, no matter what the weather. He had a little house built for him the year before at the Forks of the Assiniboine, where he had planted a garden, set out plants and flowers, and made it a little bower of beauty; but he had lived in it only one summer, for an impecunious English couple, who needed a roof to cover them rather urgently, had taken possession of it during his absence, and the kind-hearted little father could not bring himself to ask them to vacate. When his friends remonstrated with him, he turned

the conversation by telling them of another and
a better Man of whom it was written that He
" had not where to lay His head."

Father O'Flynn was greeted with delight, by
the younger ones especially. The seven little
Breezes were very demonstrative, and Thomas
Shouldice resolved to warn their father against
the priest's malign influence. He recalled a sentence or two from " Maria Monk," which said
something like this : " Give us a child until he
is ten years old, and let us teach him our doctrine, and he's ours for evermore."

" Oh, they're deep ones, them Jesuits !"

Father O'Flynn was just in time for the
" walk."

" Do you know what an Orange walk is,
father?" one of the American women asked,
really looking for information.

" Yes, daughter, yes," the little priest answered, a shadow coming into his merry grey
eyes. He gave her an evasive reply, and then
murmured to himself, as he picked a handful of
orange lilies: " It is an institution of the Evil
One to sow discord among brothers."

The walk began.

First came the fife and drum, skirling out an
Orange tune, at which the little priest winced
visibly. Then followed Thomas Shouldice, in
the guise of King William. He was mounted on
his own old, spavined grey mare, that had per-

formed this honorable office many times in her youth. But now she seemed lacking in the pride that befits the part. Thomas himself was gay with ribbons and a short red coat, whose gilt braid was sadly tarnished. One of the Yankees had kindly loaned a mottled buggy-robe for the saddle-cloth.

Behind Thomas marched the twenty-three-verse soloist and the other faithful few, followed by the seven Breeze boys, gay with yellow streamers made from the wrapping of a ham.

The Yankees grouped about were sorry to see so few in the procession. They had brought along three or four of their band instruments to furnish music if it were needed. As the end of the procession passed them, two of the smaller boys swung in behind the last two Breezes.

It was an inspiration. Instantly the whole company stepped into line—two by two, men, women, and children, waving their bunches of lilies!

Thomas, from his point of vantage, could see the whole company following his lead, and his heart swelled with pride. Under the arch the procession swept, stepping to the music, the significance of which most of the company did not even guess at—good-natured, neighborly, filled with the spirit of the West, that ever seeks to help along.

THE WAY OF THE WEST

Everyone, even Father O'Flynn, was happier than James Shewfelt, the drummer.

The fifer paused, preparatory to changing the tune. It was the drummer's opportunity. "Onward. Christian Soldiers," he sang, tapping the rhythm on the drum. The fifer caught the strain Not a voice was silent, and unconsciously hand clasped hand, and the soft afternoon air reverberated with the swelling cadence:

"We are not divided,
All one body we."

When the verse was done the fifer led off into another and another. The little priest's face glowed with pleasure. "It is the Spirit of the Lord," he whispered to himself, as he marched to the rhythm, his hand closely held by the smallest Breeze boy, whose yellow streamers and profuse decoration of orange lilies were at strange variance with his companion's priestly robes. But on this day nothing was at variance The spirit of the West was upon them, unifying, mellowing, harmonizing all conflicting emotions —the spirit of the West that calls on men everywhere to be brothers and lend a hand.

The Church of England minister did make a speech, but not the one he had intended. Instead of denominationalism, he spoke of brotherhood; instead of religious intolerance, he spoke of religious liberty; instead of the Prince of

222

Orange, who crossed the Boyne to give religious freedom to Ireland, he told of the Prince of Peace, who died on the cross to save the souls of men of every nation and kindred and tribe.

In the hush that followed Father O'Flynn stepped forward and said he thanked the brother who had planned this meeting; he was glad, he said, for such an opportunity for friends and neighbors to meet; he spoke of the glorious heritage that all had in this great new country, and how all must stand together as brothers. All prejudices of race and creed and doctrine die before the wonderful power of loving service. "The West," he said, "is the home of loving hearts and neighborly kindness, where all men's good is each man's care. For myself," he went on, "I have but one wish, and that is to be the servant of all, to be the ambassador of Him who went about doing good, and to teach the people to love honor and virtue, and each other." Then, raising his hands, he led the company in that prayer that comes ever to the lips of man when all other prayers seem vain—that prayer that we can all fall back on in our sore need:

"Our Father, who art in heaven,
Hallowed be Thy name,
Thy Kingdom come."

Two hours later a tired but happy and united company sat down to supper on the grass. At the head of the table sat Thomas Shouldice, radiating good-will. A huge white pitcher of steaming golden coffee was in his hand. He poured a cup of it brimming full, and handed it to the little priest, who sat near him.

" Have some coffee, father?" he said.

Where could such a scene as this be enacted—a Twelfth of July celebration where a Roman Catholic priest was the principal speaker, where the company dispersed with the singing of " God Save the King," led by an American band?

Nowhere, but in the Northwest of Canada, that illimitable land, with its great sunlit spaces, where the west wind, bearing on its bosom the spices of a million flowers, woos the heart of man with a magic spell and makes him kind and neighborly and brotherly!

CPSIA information can be obtained at www.ICGtesting.com
Printed in the USA
239310LV00004B/26/P

9 781177 475174